RIGHTEOUS SOUL GROWTH

SEONG JU CHOI

AuthorHouse™
1663 Liberty Drive
Bloomington, IN 47403
www.authorhouse.com
Phone: 1 (800) 839-8640

Because of the dynamic nature of the Internet, any web addresses or links contained in
this book may have changed since publication and may no longer be valid. The views
expressed in this work are solely those of the author and do not necessarily reflect the views
of the publisher, and the publisher hereby disclaims any responsibility for them.

Any people depicted in stock imagery provided by Getty Images are models,
and such images are being used for illustrative purposes only.
Certain stock imagery © Getty Images.

This book is printed on acid-free paper.

ISBN: 978-1-7283-2880-5 (sc)
ISBN: 978-1-7283-2881-2 (e)

Published by AuthorHouse 09/24/2019

Print information available on the last page.

Published by AuthorHouse 09/24/2019

authorHOUSE®

Righteous soul grows based on wicked soul being 1/ and mind 1/ in an actor cosmos

Seong ju Choi/ Monk water

Preface

This book will be used knowledge from 12 books writing. So then wicked soul definition and righteous soul definition and mind definition will be clear, this book purpose is three living actor make clear to help living in the macro concept world. In the micro concept and macro concept world, so that macro concept world is mind, micro concept world is wicked soul living in destination of wicked soul, from righteous soul living in destination place righteous soul living actors.

Righteous soul is real living, truly there is no, just righteous soul living. But micro concept world and macro concept world is cosmos in an actor living. An actor of Cosmos space is macro concept world and micro concept world. An actor of cosmos components are macro concept world seen world, seen world living of body, even unseen but actually goes with body, mind; role of wicked soul, righteous soul who is not as mind 1/, but as mind is 1/, from micro concept world righteous soul of righteous soul living in destination place and wicked soul of wicked soul living in destination place.

An actor of cosmos; here is actor is real living actor of righteous soul, Righteous soul can live in cosmos, but wicked soul is do not know cosmos but just only part of living, just easy living using do not know righteous soul role, but only to be easy obstacles are all is removed target, because wicked soul all deceit ignorance living actor, even righteous soul and wicked soul, mind level all, so that professional at wicked of deceit other, but also mind of macro concept world, then macro concept world all know to make money, that is all of time consuming behavior.

The only an actor cosmos all governing is righteous soul living actor, the actor know that so that in an actor of cosmos manage actor as strong righteous soul is cosmos, micro cosmos, micro cosmos is convergence to the 1/ righteous soul is time and space is micro cosmos, so long an actor of cosmos basic components are "body, mind, wicked soul, righteous soul, and macro concept world and micro concept world. This micro cosmos is same role is the cosmos living.

Micro concept world also moving energy is mutually interaction to live possible, this inter action is "mind body wicked soul, and righteous souls" these is flows righteous soul but resistance of wicked soul, disturb to runs to the righteous soul living in destination place, truly righteous soul is running to the righteous soul living destination place but wicked soul is role of resistance righteous soul running obstacles.

This is real important in the cosmos, real living of righteous soul is traveling from micro to macro, so that this traveling space is cosmos, so then just wicked soul is traveling obstacles, so long uses less living is living because a micro cosmos manager is only righteous soul living actor. Truly an actor cosmos traveler is only righteous soul, but all of other is righteous soul cosmos components only, so then righteous soul living itself is know the principle of an actor of cosmos.

This book will go an actor micro concept world living, of micro cosmos righteous soul traveling writing.

August 30 2018 hearing broadcasting from righteous soul living in destination place, so that I will add to preface

Righteous soul decision breath is same time, but also cosmos law is same also. So that righteous soul is survive in the macro concept world and micro concept world.

Cosmos law court is judge result is righteous soul living "it shares time with other, help other and doing real love other" is in the cosmos law, so that there is no sin, and crime so that righteous soul living is very safe.

But wicked soul easy living using "revenge and break", this decision and breath then cosmos law judge is sin and crime, so that wicked soul living is get wicked soul living energy to be falling to wicked soul living in destination place, truly wicked soul just for a while being going well but in the end reach at failure.

Mind living of getting much more than other is also doing not living of righteous soul living "it shares time with other, help other but also doing real love other", so that cosmos law court judge result is getting all of righteous soul energy is decreased but also increased wicked soul living in destination place, so then mind level living actor do not living in righteous soul then, in the end, at fist deceit from wicked soul living actor so that losing mind living, but also in the end being wicked soul the living in the end reach at the wicked soul living in destination falling.

Righteous soul decision breath is coincidence so that, righteous soul living is not macro concept world influence but all is micro concept world living, Righteous soul living decision is as getting righteous soul living energy increased then righteous soul living decision is natural, righteous soul living decision is automatically "it shares time with other, help other but also doing real love other" so that righteous soul living decision and breath is keep righteous soul living energy increased, this is very important to righteous soul living.

2018.8.30

So then righteous soul me living is as reach at the "righteous soul & nothing" then Righteous soul ≥ wicked soul so that perfectly righteous soul feeling of "clean clear of peace", if righteous soul me is living "the poor & righteous soul" then "righteous soul ≤ wicked soul" in this case still major is wicked soul but also, just equal (=) of time being feeling of righteous soul so that still it is not perfect safer of righteous soul living.

So that "the poor & righteous soul" see wicked soul, hearing of wicked soul so that the living is mixed with wicked soul and righteous soul, this living is righteous soul living is in the corner of living, that is safer from wicked soul living "revenge and break", truly this is seen in the macro and micro concept world living, so that this is at first righteous soul me seen in me as the "thinking of wicked soul" but also in the macro concept world all of follow of "think of wicked soul" so that in the macro concept world living are wicked soul living.

As the see in the micro concept me then "think of wicked soul" try to keep doing "revenge and break" endless suppled to do "revenge and break" so then so huge fear of wicked soul living.

But as grown to "righteous soul & nothing", here is "righteous soul= nothing" so that as the righteous soul "nothing" so that automatically wicked soul is disperse, then in this pace living of "nothing", here is noting is there is no righteous soul, and wicked soul, but this is "righteous soul & nothing" is must be righteous soul being "Righteous soul ≥ wicked soul" so then right after " righteous soul & nothing", because righteous soul living originality purpose is running to the righteous soul living in destination place, so that as the approach to the micro concept world of righteous soul living, then it must be "Righteous soul ≥ wicked soul" in the end being "righteous soul & nothing", then automatically only righteous soul living safe returning to the righteous soul living in destination place reaching.

Righteous soul = wicked soul create clean clear of peace is possible

Righteous soul "the poor & righteous soul" is "righteous soul ≤ wicked soul"

This living in the macro concept world feeling is seen wicked soul, hear of wicked soul also, so that even living in righteous soul me but see in the macro concept world

Righteous soul "righteous soul & nothing" is "Righteous soul ≥ wicked soul"

This living in the macro concept world feeling is do not seen wicked soul, do not hearing of wicked soul, so that as living of "righteous soul me" living is perfect righteous soul living in the macro concept world.

All of macro concept world seen and hearing is image of "righteous soul ≤ wicked soul" because all of living is in me not out of me, but all is micro and macro concept world boundary living only, just wicked soul strong then all of images are all seen, but also this image as the real, but as the "Righteous soul ≥ wicked soul" then there is no any image but all living is "righteous soul & nothing" so that truly "nothing" is real.

"Righteous soul ≥ wicked soul" create feeing of "clean clear of peace", this is being " righteous soul & nothing"

As the righteous soul and nothing, is macro concept world all is seen righteous soul, all hearing is righteous soul. This is righteous soul only living is "nothing" so that "righteous soul & nothing" living is "clean clear of peace"

My macro concept world righteous soul me new slogan is "clean clear of peace" this is all of world in the macro concept world is all is being seen is "righteous soul living actors" so then now living is all living creature of righteous soul living actors.

As "righteous soul living me" is now "righteous soul & nothing" so that righteous soul me feeling "clean clear of peace".

From now on macro concept world real living of righteous soul me living is not seen wicked soul, not hear of wicked soul, as living of "righteous soul & nothing" so that there is "Righteous soul ≥ wicked soul", so then macro concept world living feeling is "clean clear of peace"

"Clean clear of peace" is real living; this mighty energy is huge bright so that all livings in the macro concept world beings are righteous soul living actors. Just there is no discriminate because there is no mind, so that righteous soul living is already there is no discriminate mind, that is nothing,

In the end righteous soul me is "righteous soul & nothing" so that truly "righteous soul me" living is "righteous soul and nothing" this living feeling is "clean clear of peace" living.

2018.9.7

Table of Contents

An actor cosmos

"Righteous soul grows based on wicked soul being 1/ and mind1/ in an actor cosmos", in this long name of book, has keywords are Righteous soul, wicked soul, mind and an actor cosmos, here an actor cosmos is not accustomed to righteous soul me.

How to explain an actor cosmos? At fist this is challenge, but I have hint then, this book name subject is "Righteous soul" so that, in this book main actor is "righteous soul" this is clear. Time and space must be required. So then time and space build, righteous soul try to use what righteous soul built concept, that is micro concept (-1/~+1/) but how to go is not sure.

Then in an actor cosmos moving energy in the cosmos is what? On today morning, in the shower it comes inferable energy is "righteous soul living behavior" "it shares time with other, help other, but also doing real love other" in this behavior doing then righteous soul living behavior energy is generation, this is righteous soul living energy.

An actor cosmos has a rule, but righteous soul me do not know now.

Righteous soul will meet a wicked soul at the micro concept world.

Righteous soul will meet a mind at macro concept world.

Righteous soul will be lived both micro concept world and macro concept world

Here is an actor cosmos will be macro concept world and micro concept world.

Still righteous soul me do not know how to solve this problems but righteous soul me believe that righteous soul will be helped from other righteous souls even much more than righteous soul living in destination place.

Actually righteous soul do not know but by accidently righteous soul me used the word of cosmos, when in my inter world, some of "think of wicked soul push in me" then righteous soul saying "right before thinking I'm forgive it and send to cosmos law court" still this is not clear but as rule what happened to me, "think of wicked soul'.

Infer that "cosmos law court" mean that some of decision working "wrong or not" even I forgive as righteous soul me, but final decision is to be end of "thinking of wicked soul".

Here is cosmos must be time and space but also ultimate by the cosmos rule, then decision function also, it is not clear but dare adventure of starting "Righteous soul grows based on wicked soul being $1/\infty$ and mind$1/\infty$ in an actor cosmos"

Micro concept and micro cosmos

Micro concept and micro cosmos,

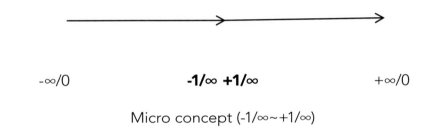

-∞/0   **-1/∞ +1/∞**   +∞/0

Micro concept (-1/∞~+1/∞)

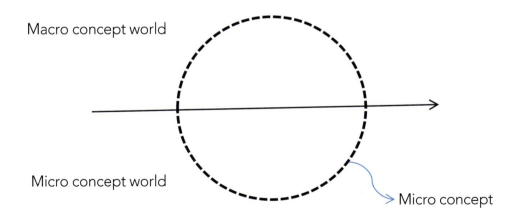

Macro concept world

Micro concept world

Micro concept

(-1/∞~+1/∞)

Micro cosmos

Righteous soul living between micro concept world and macro concept world, micro concept point is in the righteous soul, an righteous soul and righteous soul living actor has micro concept point (-1/∞~+1/∞), Righteous soul living is real living, truth living. Righteous soul lives between micro and macro, and macro and micro all circulation, Righteous soul travel from micro to macro, but also adverse direction of macro to micro.

Micro concept (-1/∞~+1/∞) is same as before and after, macro concept world and micro concept world is same.

Micro concept is much more than smaller than righteous soul, because righteous soul also smaller of 1/∞. So long righteous soul and micro concept is essential structure. If infer of living structure both micro concept world and macro concept world.

Micro concept world structure

Righteous soul + micro concept (-1/∞ ~+1/∞) communicate and recognition among Righteous souls, but also righteous soul living in destination place, recognition through micro concept certify. Micro concept (-1/∞~+1/∞) this is path, tunnel, road, and "it shares time with other, and help other and but also do real love" to be this all of problems solving through micro concept(-1/∞~+1/∞). Micro concept point is communication macro to micro, and macro righteous soul to micro concept world righteous soul living souls.

Macro concept world structure

Righteous soul living actor + micro concept(-1/∞~+1/∞), righteous soul living actor is living in macro concept world, then living in macro concept world living actors. Then how to communication and recognition is only micro concept point, the communication recognition between macro to micro is through micro concept point(-1/∞~+1/∞).

Righteous soul use micro concept($-1/\infty \sim +1/\infty$), micro concept is moving between micro and macro, reversed direction also.

Micro cosmos

Macro and micro concept space is micro concept cosmos, so that in this micro cosmos has rules, this rule is cosmos order. So that micro cosmos rule is governing in the micro cosmos. Probably in the living of macro concept world, righteous soul living me, whenever "think of wicked soul surge up" then righteous soul me " right before thinking I forgive and send to the cosmos law court" to be all clean clear.

Micro cosmos, macro concept world and micro concept world all both governed by the law of micro cosmos.

So then "the think of wicked soul invader me" then " righteous soul me forgive think of wicked soul then send to micro cosmos law court" then it clean clear of think of wicked soul invader righteous soul me.

Righteous soul + micro concept($-1/\infty \sim +1/\infty$) then this living is in the road to the righteous soul living in destination place.

Truly Righteous soul + micro concept ($-1/\infty +1/\infty$) living in the micro cosmos, then to be rule in the micro cosmos, then in this cosmos, righteous soul runs to the righteous soul living in destination place, this is real living.

But while righteous soul voyage then this voyage tour route is righteous soul living in destination place going, then all depend on micro concept ($-1/\infty \sim +1/\infty$), wicked soul living "revenge and breaking" so that in the micro concept world in the same place living. But micro concept is only living in righteous soul, but also righteous soul living meet mind in the macro concept world.

While both micro macro concept world voyage, then righteous soul micro concept survive then, righteous soul use micro concept to communicate righteous soul living in destination place " it shared time with other, help other but also dong real love other" of being righteous soul behavior of target, then make possible travel safe to the righteous soul living in destination place.

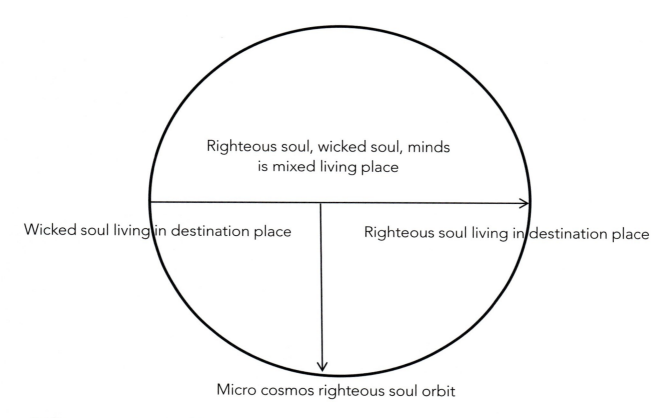

Righteous soul, wicked soul, minds
is mixed living place

Wicked soul living in destination place

Righteous soul living in destination place

Micro cosmos righteous soul orbit

Righteous soul is real living

So then righteous soul living orbit between micro concept world and micro concept world

Start voyage micro concept world macro concept world

Righteous soul Righteous soul + wicked soul Righteous soul + wicked soul + mind +body

Macro concept world micro concept world righteous soul living in destination place

Righteous soul +body Righteous soul Righteous soul

This is micro cosmos orbit, all of orbit, then all of communication through micro concept $(-1/\infty \sim +1/\infty)$.

Righteous soul real living safe returning to the righteous soul living in destination place is so urgent, the all of living is using micro concept $(-1/\infty \sim +1/\infty)$, infer of if follow of micro concept then righteous soul can use micro concept then communicate with righteous soul living in destination place, then righteous soul voyage will be safe so then safe returning possible.

Infer that micro concept make possible keep a rule of micro cosmos, then not be broken rule, keep helping through micro concept, because righteous soul living in destination place give correction voyage regular line.

Keep a rule of micro cosmos and helping from righteous soul living in destination place with micro concept$(-1/\infty \sim +1/\infty$" then righteous soul voyage safe returning is possible.

Righteous soul growth with "mind 1/∞"

Righteous soul, Righteous living in destination place, Righteous soul creation, Righteous soul safe retuning from macro concept world to righteous soul living in destination place, righteous soul mission in the voyage macro concept world, Righteous soul living behavior "it shares time with other, help other, and doing real love other" but strong is "Righteous soul growth with "mind 1/∞"" is so strong.

Macro concept world, mind level living actors are living for "getting much more than others", this is macro concept world safe living getting. So that majority of living actors are living in the macro concept world, this living actors are free mind level living actors are going with mind ∞, who criticize, no one just all live to be "getting much more than other".

So all of doing then plus mind is mixed, so that mind is strong, original purpose doing is expect original result.

But original purpose doing + mind= do not getting original result. Because original purpose used energy for it, then result will be comes original result, but as the original purpose doing +mind, energy is robbed from "mind" so that original purpose doing 60% + mind40%= it is not reach at original result.

In the mind level living actors hard to get result, infer that in the macro concept world all mind1/∞ then reach at the purpose result, so that this is righteous soul appeared, righteous soul get knowledge from righteous soul living in destination place.

Original purpose doing 100% + mind 1/∞, as the mind is about to zero, then the place appeared by righteous soul, so then righteous soul behavior is "it shares time with other, help other, but also doing real love other" then righteous soul living actor " original purpose doing 100% + righteous soul of ""it shares time with other, help other, but also doing real love other" then to get original purpose, then all of problems solving by helping righteous soul living in destination place.

Righteous soul living as mind is $1/\infty$, in the macro concept world is so strong, so that righteous soul is so hard going with body, because "mind +body" just one, truly this is not, so then "mind +body" then mind" do getting much more than others" so that "body" just do all time used for mind order "getting much more than other', truly "mind$1/\infty$ +righteous soul +body' then

Mind +body= Body behavior 60%+ mind 40%= then body must be 60% is 100%, then mind getting 40% so that body over behavior, so that Body living is robbed from mind.

As mind$1/\infty$,

Righteous soul + body= Body behavior 100% + righteous soul "it shares time with other, help other, but also doing real love other"= Body behavior 100% energy is all used original purpose, but Body also be righteous soul behavior of helping from righteous soul living in destination place.

As the righteous soul +body, so then body is not used for the salver for "getting much more than other" but with righteous soul living body is fully enough body sustainment but also support role, the excitement living of "it shares time with other, help other but also doing real love other" then body time is not robbed from "mind".

In the macro concept world

Mind is all wrong doer, but in the living of macro concept world, no one know it, because getting much more is mind, this is possible to the macro concept world living actor, but truly macro concept world living well, here is living well is "water floor down living' is all is not mind level living actors, but infer that somehow enlighten all of their, all effort then in the end getting enlighten then, the enlighten is get used micro concept "$-1/\infty \sim +1/\infty$", so then in righteous soul living in destination place do righteous soul behavior "it shares time with other, help other, but also dong real love other'.

Macro concept world living happened as mind1/∞, then the moment righteous soul is appeared then can use micro concept (-1/∞~+1/∞) this is the tunnel, gate to bring back problems solving knowledge, so called creation of knowledge getting from righteous soul living in destination place.

In the mind level living to righteous soul living is so long time required, someone do not reach at righteous soul, all of living mind level living and finish in the macro concept world, but also do not living in excitement of righteous soul living, creation of knowledge getting from micro concept "-1/∞~+1/∞", this is all possible as mind1/∞, this is possible is so peak in hard time, or just try to solve the problems, then if mind is moment disappeared, this is micro concept "-1/∞~+1/∞" then appear up of righteous soul living actor.

Righteous soul living actor living hearing broadcasting from righteous soul living in destination place, all of broadcasting is creation of knowledge for running to the righteous soul living in destination place. Righteous soul living is all of time is micro concept "-1/∞~+1/∞" this is the way to the righteous soul living in destination place.

Infer that righteous soul me is dot of micro concept "-1/∞~+1/∞" this is regular line to the righteous soul living in destination place.

"-1/∞~+1/∞"

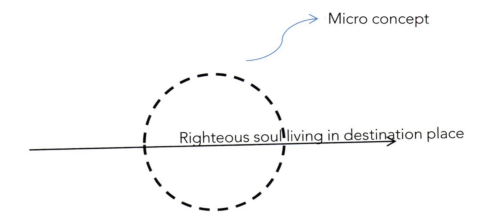

Micro concept

Righteous soul living in destination place

Runs voyage

Micro cosmos

But mind living is blocked micro concept, so that living in mind "getting much more than other" this is safe living. But also it don't necessary mind level living is all, so then mind level living actor living is all not true.

So that to be feeling all of getting, but also try to getting, but that is not satisfied, but righteous soul living actor is excitement with "the poor & righteous soul" "righteous soul & nothing", righteous soul open to communicate from righteous soul living in destination place.

Righteous soul living is based on mind1/∞, so then righteous soul do not living for "getting much more than others" but do living righteous soul living behavior ' it shares time with others" just do righteous soul living mission carry out.

Righteous soul voyage mission is "find lover make righteous soul bring safe back to the righteous soul living in destination place"

Infer of if righteous soul me fully living, then righteous soul me do mission " a lover making righteous soul" then macro concept world being spared righteous soul, but also each one save from mind level to righteous soul, then, macro concept world possible living mind1/∞, so that it don't have to "getting much more than others".

Righteous soul living is automatically being target of "other righteous soul shares with me, and help me, then other righteous soul do real love me" this is righteous soul me living in excitement in the macro concept world.

Righteous soul living of mind1/∞, then righteous soul me see, without mind, then all of creature of nature beauty is so excitement, this is what I dreamed in the micro concept world, so righteous soul living is doing real living without mind all used up time for getting much more than others.

Macro concept world mind living

Macro mind living is mind∞, there is no break. If this living is accept then, it must be wrong, so then if macro concept world mind∞ must be recognition then it comes to the mind∞, here is an actor cosmos, or micro cosmos all know an actor of mind∞, that is break rule of an actor cosmos. So then an actor or micro cosmos break it. So that mind∞ is limited mind living.

Mind in the micro cosmos it never break balance so that it has rhythm, in the cosmos rule is up and down.

But mind +body, mind is doing not accept cosmos rule, if full then be empty. This is cosmos rule. So then mind must be make full, so then after full another full, mind is full +full +full= full, but righteous soul living is all "it shares time with other, help other, but also do real love other" so that righteous soul is not full, it always being in empty living, because righteous soul living is running to the righteous soul living in destination place, righteous soul living is voyage in an micro cosmos, so that it is so safe living.

Macro concept world mind living is "getting much more than other" it is same mind is "full +full +full= full".

Mind all of effort to getting much more than other

Here is righteous soul is will accept "the poor & righteous soul" "righteous soul & nothing" living possible.

Macro concept world mind∞, then micro cosmos rule "full and empty", then "up And down"

Mind∞ = "without being empty but keep full, without down but keep up"

This is not an actor cosmos rule, but also micro cosmos rule.

Righteous soul mind 1/∞ is = righteous soul appear in an actor so then micro concept "-1/∞~+1/∞" also appeared so that righteous soul keep a rule of micro cosmos rule, and communicate with righteous soul living in destination place of micro concept world.

Then righteous soul living in "the poor & righteous soul" "righteous soul & nothing" but living "it shares time with other, and help other, but also doing real love other' then reverse other of righteous soul behavior is same to me, so that righteous soul living is keep harmony in keep a rule of micro cosmos rule.

But Macro concept world mind living

Do not know, righteous soul living of creation of knowledge. "the poor & righteous soul" "righteous soul & nothing" this living is keep running to the righteous soul living in destination place.

Macro concept world mind living, mind∞ is impossible full +full +full= full is impossible.

If mind do know, not to be full then not to be up, then do not reach at full, then it must be not full + not full + not full= not full is possible of keeping an micro cosmos rule within so that mind can live possible " to get much more than others" but if reach at full then, in this point also adopt to " to get much more than other" then what happened in a law of cosmos, this is do not reach at full but righteous soul living of "it shares time with other and help other but also doing real love" this rule is within in micro concept cosmos, then this rule is not kept by mind in the macro concept world, then cosmos rule give judgement penalty.

Here cosmos rule penalty actor is "wicked soul", wicked soul living actor is "easy living" and to be possible wicked soul has strong energy of "revenge and break", this target is "mind∞ is impossible full +full +full= full"

So that mind∞ is full is combined to "mind +wicked soul" if comes wicked soul to mind∞, then mind do not know micro concept world wicked soul, so that at first wicked soul visit is good to the mind, because wicked soul is used by mind∞ to fulfil of "full +full +full= full possible" but also with wicked soul it keep continued full is strong creating full, so that mind∞ keep use wicked soul "easy living" and "revenge and break", but somehow after, mind∞ disappeared, then wicked soul is occupied instead of mind∞, then mind ∞ disappeared.

Infer that

Wicked soul "easy living" using "revenge and break energy using"

Mind∞ full +full +full= full, still time all used for much more than others even use wicked soul energy

Mind living "to get much more than other" all of time used up but is keep a rule of actor cosmos

Not full of keep "the poor & righteous soul" is in the lowest place keep in micro cosmos rule with micro concept "-1/∞ ~+1/∞" communicate with righteous soul living in destination place, then keep running to the righteous soul living in destination place.

Macro concept world mind living's only pleasure is "getting much more than other", to keep pleasure but that is not limitless going up, going full, so this ways keep pleasure is impossible because that is beyond of micro cosmos rule, so that this is wicked soul living of "revenge and break region".

Macro concept world righteous soul me living

Righteous soul me just do forgive doing with me but all is done by cosmos law court. So that all I know forgive and love my lover all, from now on my lover is all innocence, my lover all being clean clear with me. "Righteous soul me" declare. This is macro concept world righteous soul me living.

Macro concept world righteous soul me living is "all forgive and doing real love others", this is righteous soul me doing only.

Macro concept world righteous soul do solve then, for the solving at first all forgive and do real love other.

This is macro concept world righteous soul living is "clean clear" in me.

"clean clear" is excitement then it is based on mind=1/∞, just righteous soul & nothing.

Macro concept world righteous soul living actor living with wicked soul, mind, righteous soul living actors, then righteous soul me doing is "just forgive living with righteous soul me, then do real love other" this is righteous soul me only doing, but after that saying that "send to the cosmos law court" then all of behavior with me, doing harm also "revenge and break me of wicked souls" all are judged in the cosmos law courts.

Cosmos law court judgement righteous soul living energy and wicked soul living penalty result. In the cosmos law court is macro, micro all of living is judged.

So that cosmos is called micro cosmos, and an actor cosmos, is same, an actor living is "righteous soul, wicked soul, and mind but also macro and micro" so that an actor cosmos saying, an actor cosmos law court judgement then the result is righteous soul living energy, or wicked soul living energy.

Macro concept world righteous soul me living is do "forgive and do real love, and other actors relationship is be sending to the cosmos law court" so then I'm just forgive and doing real love is macro concept world doing only.

Macro concept world righteous soul me being possible all "forgive and do real love other", so that righteous soul me all the time righteous soul me do forgive and do real love other, so then righteous soul me living is "clean clear" and excitement living.

How to feel in excitement as living in Righteous soul

Righteous soul living is not grow living in wicked soul and mind level living. Righteous soul excitement is not in macro concept world, but in the micro concept world. Righteous soul living in excitement is macro concept world feeling is "clean clear without cloudy in me".

Righteous soul is bringing creature of knowledge, this is also feeling in excitement. Righteous soul living in super in excitement is solving the problems helping from righteous soul meet though micro concept micro concept world righteous soul living in destination place.

Righteous soul appear and safe living is mind is $1/\infty$, then it is momentum of so huge excitement. This is righteous soul birth and growing in me.

Righteous soul is wicked soul $1/\infty$ is also feel safe righteous soul urgent disappeared or not, so then wicked soul is $1/\infty$ is safe living in righteous soul.

Righteous soul living behavior is "it shares time with other, help other, but also doing real love other"

Righteous soul is doing real living, living in cosmos law, if living in righteous soul then kept law so that accumulate righteous soul living energy.

Righteous soul living is also cosmos law with natural living, just living then automatically running to the righteous soul living in destination place.

Righteous soul can live making condition doing: "the poor & righteous soul" is both wicked soul "easy living" mind "getting much more than others", so then both wicked soul, mind, space out is "the poor & righteous soul"

Righteous soul safe from wicked soul, being disappeared to the wicked soul of "righteous soul & nothing", this is righteous soul living, growing harvest, then before safe returning to the righteous soul living in destination place.

Righteous soul living is basic voice, which is from righteous soul living, righteous soul original sound from righteous soul then, this do, make other be peace.

Righteous soul living is living as creator creating purpose living of role playing. Then creator will see all of righteous soul living turning back to the righteous soul living in destination place.

Righteous soul will do communicate with righteous soul creator, then creator keep sent to righteous soul to make runs direction and all of running make safe, so that righteous soul can hear from creator of righteous souls

Righteous soul do live in mission carry "do find lover who living wicked soul, then do use doing real love then wicked soul of lover make righteous soul, and then carry to the righteous soul living in destination place"

While so huge righteous soul living is make possible righteous soul me, making excitement is "clean clear" to be that righteous soul me, keep doing "forgive and doing real love", righteous soul me wicked soul did "revenge break other" this living all of sins make zero, then creating of righteous soul so for the wicked soul me, so then "all of time think of wicked soul surge up" then right time, righteous soul me "do forgive thinking of wicked soul"

Righteous soul in the cosmos so then macro and micro concept world so then, righteous soul living is voyage start from micro to now macro but also same safe returning to the righteous soul living in destination place.

Created in the righteous soul living, then created righteous soul is growing in the macro concept world, righteous soul living in grow, "the poor & righteous soul" "righteous soul

& nothing" then safe returning to the righteous soul living in destination place, then safe returning righteous soul living in eternity in the righteous soul living.

In the macro concept world this is how feel in excitement, macro concept world righteous soul is growing time, learning time, to all of living in the righteous souls, even all of living actors are being pure of righteous souls, so then in the righteous soul living in destination living is so excitement living, for this righteous soul me, how to be living in the macro concept world, is it don't have to question to me, so then it must be living in the macro concept world righteous soul living be hard, please do not be living in "easy living" "getting much more than other" righteous soul is now living in growing so that, while growing is overcoming and learning and please do righteous soul living is running to the righteous soul living in destination place.

Righteous soul me running to the righteous soul living in destination place is do not lose running road is also feeing in excitement, but also keep growing righteous soul living.

Righteous soul me is feeling in excitement is keep growing, keep making better me, this is righteous soul me living in excitement, truly now is so excitement in writing on righteous soul growing what I really wanted writing.

Righteous soul me doing is simple "it shares time with other, help other, but also doing real love other" it is righteous soul me is heard broadcasting from righteous soul living in destination place, so that in the macro concept world living behavior is from righteous soul living in destination place truth.

Righteous soul living feel in excitement is other living of righteous soul living, when I read the book of pre runners of righteous soul living actors trace book of righteous souls, it is also so feeling in excitement to righteous soul me.

While keep writing righteous soul growing then, righteous soul me being in getting excitement to me, truly righteous soul living in macro concept world, all the time wicked soul temptation to me "hey living is simple getting much more than other" then you can live with us, this is very simple, you have to live in same mind with me do not going with righteous soul, truly your living is not knowing so hard why you live in hard, please living with us simple/

But also wicked soul is huge string try to break; this wicked soul has the strong arms, "revenge and break energy" so that righteous soul strong distance from wicked soul so that do not living in "easy living" in the easy living space sure of wicked soul is living, so that righteous soul living me is living in "the poor and righteous soul", righteous soul me living is not "easy living" so then wicked soul temptation to live "easy living".

Righteous soul living is "the poor & righteous soul" so that righteous soul living is excitement, macro concept world poor living is lonesome, fear because the poor me is perfectly segregate from majority, the poor is not seen but also, how to do now writing, it must be the poor living is so hard, "the poor & righteous soul" is not merely "poor" but righteous soul, this is huge difference, righteous soul me is in "the poor & righteous soul" yes, now living in macro concept world I'm sorry god, god help me so that living safe, sorry may be sorry, but righteous soul me is "the poor & righteous soul me", thank you god, yet actually righteous soul me is not beggar of the poor, but my living is can live in the home, and eat 3 times a day.

But even though righteous soul me living is "the poor & righteous soul" righteous soul me has motto is "I will not get my own", "I will not be fear of being the poor", this is string against to the mind living of "getting much more than other"

As living mind then, righteous soul me already disappeared, so that not living of righteous soul, but mind level me is keeping living of getting hurry much more than others, so that righteous soul me living is "the poor & righteous soul" this is safe living of righteous soul living.

Righteous soul growing is so excitement, because righteous soul is what I wanted to write, so that righteous soul me living is now naturally being excitement because there is no variants of wicked soul and mind living.

Righteous soul living is going deeper living place, righteous soul living is almost not seen, but the time and space is righteous soul living, the righteous soul living is must be giving me in the broadcasting then, righteous soul me all just write down from righteous soul me, helping me of problems then it must be excitement writing this book.

Righteous soul is now must know is "creating in the righteous soul living in destination place, to learn and grow in the macro concept world living and running to the righteous soul living in destination place with do mission carry find lover of wicked soul, making lover righteous soul then with love safe returning to the righteous soul living in destination place.

Righteous soul living in excitement

Living in excitement & Righteous soul living in excitement, in the macro concept world living, it going floor down is must be inferring that "feeing in excitement", most time is occupied by living in excitement.

Excitement is almost living of routine, to be real and righteous soul living in excitement is need time to be living in real excitement, this is true, but why righteous soul me, seeking in excitement.

What is excitement?

Excitement infer that

Start ⟶ Excitement

Start ⟶ Excitement

Start ⟶ Excitement

Excitement is must be result of all start. If I do not feeling in excitement then, it must be now start region, so that it required to me wait to be being excitement.

Excitement is must be righteous soul living actor's energy, this excitement is must be result then this is promotion motive and engine to go for the righteous soul living in destination place.

Excitement is mixed with even clear of result, but excitement is creation of knowledge truth living result, excitement is all of micro concept "-1/∞~+1/∞", why recently I haven't feeling in excitement.

Righteous soul can live without being excitement?

Cause of excitement is reach a conclusion of existing problem solving, so then righteous soul me infer that out of living in righteous soul, righteous soul seek in known to other who read what I wrote book, whether I do not know that.

Righteous soul living in excitement

Excitement is all mixed with righteous soul living

Mind is 1/∞ in the time and space appeared "righteous soul"

But mind is still living then; righteous soul is must be dim, then seen mind of living "getting much more than other".

As appeared up of mind then there is feeling in excitement.

Feeling in excitement with living in micro concept -1/∞~+1/∞, this is mind is 1/∞.

How to feel in excitement?

Here is make mind 1/∞, this is what macro concept me can doing, mind is strong combined to body, so then mind and body detach is then attach righteous soul with body.

Without mind then the living is living of righteous soul living. Righteous soul living is living in "creation of knowledge of truth" then all of function is going with righteous soul of micro concept -1/∞~+1/∞.

Truly micro concept cosmos is lie in the micro concept -1/∞~+1/∞, righteous soul living is in the micro concept time and space -1/∞~+1/∞, living in excitement is circulation of living, is keep running as living of righteous soul living, how to get this energy or concentration of living, but righteous soul must be being "revenger and breaking" by wicked soul living.

Excitement living being "be revenge and break", if disappeared excitement then, in the place wicked soul "easy living" is occupied, this is feeling is "winning is excitement, lose is do not excitement', getting easy living then other must be losing actor. This is macro concept world living of coincidence of mind getting much more than other, but also doing easy living is all fulfillments, so that this is feeling in easy living of excitement.

But wicked soul, mind feeling in excitement is based on filling in space, to be filling is this must be living of divergence ∞ living, this is impossible, but some of winning excitement is very moment because still divergence the end is not comes in macro concept world living.

Righteous soul excitement

Micro concept world living in the time and space of micro concept -1/∞~+1/∞, the time and space is in creation of knowledge, so then macro concept world living righteous soul me excitement living is getting creation of knowledge truth.

Righteous soul me excitement

Start writing Excitement

To be feeling in righteous soul living in excitement is doing keeping endless writing is excitement.

Righteous soul living in excitement is eternity living of excitement. Macro concept world "mind" and "wicked soul" to be easy living, then their excitement living is 'computer game" this is battle game to revenge and break so that mind and wicked souls are all excitement with computer game, here is not, this is macro concept world, must be this is so easy living, to be excitement this is anything related with creation of knowledge and truth living.

Righteous soul of excitement living is growing of righteous souls

Macro concept world seen world, an actor also grow in the physical, the same as micro concept world righteous soul also keep growing, righteous soul created in the micro concept world righteous soul living in destination place, then living in cultivating in the macro concept world, the time and space are mixed with mind and wicked soul and righteous souls, so that living macro concept world, righteous soul me must be grow keep a rule of micro cosmos, so that righteous soul living is clean clear of living.

Righteous soul me to be feel in excitement is all cover of keep a rule of micro concept cosmos law is first, the keep doing bring creation of knowledge from righteous soul living in destination place, then do mission meet lover do real love lover then being both survive in the macro concept world, living in excitement then safe returning to the righteous soul living in destination place.

Righteous soul circulation created in the micro concept world, then growing in the macro concept world then in the end safe returning to the micro concept world of righteous soul living in destination place. This is finished circulation of living under the micro concept world cosmos law, righteous soul survive in the macro concept world then safe returning then, the time and space is wait living in eternity in the righteous soul living in destination place.

Righteous soul grows feeing in excitement.

Righteous soul and excitement is engine of living in the macro concept world "the poor & righteous soul" and "righteous soul & nothing" because this living is has all of temptation to revenge and breaking, so that righteous soul living grow is battle filed in the micro concept.

Righteous soul living in excitement is overcoming of any attacking from wicked soul and mind level living actors because righteous soul feeling in excitement is so excitement, it must be wicked soul easy living is not compare with righteous soul living in excitement, because righteous soul me living is based on creating knowledge of truth real living, but also if keep living In macro concept world, the righteous soul me is keep growth righteous soul living, all grown righteous soul living eternity in the righteous soul living in destination place.

Righteous soul living excitement is living in circulation of micro cosmos orbital space, so then this orbital is endless circulation, this is not disappeared of truth, so that righteous soul me is keep living in creature of knowledge of truth that is micro concept line, micro concept line same as micro cosmos orbital.

Righteous soul survive and safe returning then, sure of keep a rule cosmos law, then do not lose of cosmos orbital, so long in the macro concept world living is righteous soul growing but also circulation of voyage micro via macro to micro of micro cosmos orbital road only recognition of micro concept -1/∞~+1/∞.

"Living excitement"

Righteous soul surviving, getting result, keeping a rule of micro cosmos, but also hearing broadcasting from righteous soul living in destination place, in the end feeling in excitement with clean clear.

Righteous soul growth first righteous

Righteous soul living is cosmos law, just real living. In the cosmos law macro micro concept world both living in main character is righteous soul. Truly righteous soul is real living, but wicked soul is role of make hard or the way of living "revenge & break" role, this living is not normal living, so that righteous soul living is true living.

How to live in righteous soul living?

Righteous soul living is first living is righteous then, the all of other living is righteous soul living, the first living is not big or huge, but just first righteous soul is so weak, so poor, feeble, but the living is righteous soul then after all of living is righteous soul living.

Righteous soul living is also clumsy, poor living but righteously living then grow, this is in the cosmos rule, then in the macro concept world, first living, "body +mind+ wicked soul+ righteous soul" in this strong mixed in components are make one of living, then just very small, feeble sprout of righteous soul is seen then the living is sure of righteous soul living all of living in the macro concept world.

Here feeble righteous soul is beginning communication through micro concept "-1/∞~+1/∞", this is also include in cosmos law, so that righteous soul living is mixed with grow, at that time is not appeared up of righteous soul, but the time is running then, righteous soul sprout keep steady growing, so then in the end the righteous soul of "the poor & righteous soul" "righteous soul & nothing" living way.

Righteous soul living is not "easy living of wicked soul" "getting much more than other of mind" so that the living is at last then "hard living, follow the cosmos law, then it shares time with other, help other but also doing real love other". But macro concept world living is also very important, then it is same as wicked soul, and mind but righteous soul living behavior is not same in the micro concept.

Wicked soul living is "main is wicked soul but to live easy living stealth getting mind, so that wicked soul +mind = wicked soul"

But mind is originality of mind is "getting much more than other" then here is getting much more is ∞, so then to get much more than other, mind be temptation using wicked soul energy "revenge and break strong power" so that "mind + wicked soul= mind"

Wicked soul and mind is common is somehow difference both use each other, then they are all lose do real living, so that the living is out of cosmos law, they are all out of cosmos orbital, then in the point of view cosmos orbital lose, then they are not count on real living.

But righteous soul is living as the mind is $1/\infty$, this is so huge principle, righteous soul living is "the poor & righteous soul", here is wicked soul "easy living" is not survive that righteous soul is pure of righteous soul being, so that righteous soul is created in the condition of mind of macro concept of strong with body, then as mind being $1/\infty$, then righteous soul is combined with body, "mind$1/\infty$+wicked soul $1/\infty$ +righteous soul= righteous soul" this is righteous soul living.

Righteous soul living is from sprout of feeble righteous soul, but righteous soul keep grown, then even wicked soul and mind is combined to be living wicked soul, and mind living but righteous soul is keep growing of righteous soul, so that righteous soul is cosmos law governing time and space of orbital of cosmos so that, in the cosmos orbital then keep communicating with righteous soul living in destination place, so then righteous soul me is cosmos voyage living also, in the micro cosmos, righteous soul me voyage is keep control from righteous soul living in destination place where righteous soul start voyage in the macro concept world and micro concept world micro cosmos voyage.

So then keep in the micro cosmos rule is right helping righteous soul living actor be safe, from other do not living is righteous soul living, righteous soul living actor do cosmos orbital voyage make possible audible frequency from righteous soul living in destination place, so called that is hearing broadcasting from righteous soul living in destination place.

How to live in righteous soul living?

Righteous soul living is in the weak of righteous soul, it must be not seen from other of macro concept world "easy living, getting much more than other" because in the macro concept world all of adults are wicked soul and mind living actors, so that the point of wicked soul and mind is not seen righteous soul living feeble.

But here is do not forget it, who live in macro concept world living actors has same start

"mind +body+ wicked soul + righteous soul" this is all of macro concept world living, this is just like compared rocket to the cosmos voyage, then righteous soul cosmos voyage orbital of cosmos then, gradually just real living, just cosmos macro and micro concept world all living possible, righteous soul, then as cosmos orbit voyage then some hot to go with "mind +body+ wicked soul + righteous soul" but as feeble of righteous soul growth then, but also righteous soul being enlighten then righteous soul is running to the righteous soul living in destination place safe retuning then, just like cosmos voyage rocket is all removed then only capsule of righteous soul is only remain so long, all of burden to the righteous soul, then being simple righteous soul only,

Then, righteous soul reach at the "righteous soul & nothing", this is real living. All of hard suffering all natural do, procedure of righteous soul is being reaches at the righteous soul living in destination place.

Feeble of righteous soul is not to be temptation from living of "Easy living" but living of righteous soul living, how to righteous soul living energy in the voyage macro concept world is "excitement" wicked soul easy living, but even hard, poor living, but in the hard and poor living also has feeling of "excitement" this excitement is hearing broadcasting from righteous soul living in destination place, then the feeling is huge excitement, but also righteous soul living in micro concept "-1/∞!+1/∞" so then through micro concept it bring to solve face problems then, righteous soul living in destination place righteous soul behavior "it shares time with other, help other, but also doing real love other', then living in macro concept world, the as living of righteous soul me is the same as macro concept world, in the micro concept world living righteous soul same shares time and helping, and doing real love, this righteous soul living actor excitement.

Oh today righteous soul me get a concept of "excitement" is excitement is not made for me excitement, but do righteous soul living behavior "it shares time with other, help other, but also doing real love other" then other of righteous soul do for me, then righteous soul me feel in excitement, if righteous soul me living in hard, and suffering living that is keep running to the righteous soul living in destination place, then in the way, "the poor & righteous soul" must be shares time with other, helped from other, but also to be real loved from others" this is feeling in "excitement'.

Wicked soul "easy living" is all of power of energy "revenge and break" use,. Other make hard then only wicked soul live in "easy living" this living is not count on, in the cosmos law, that is perfect not to be impossible for the righteous soul living in destination place.

Mind level living actor also to be "getting much more than other" they do not know "it shares time with other, help other, but also doing real love other", but only mind level living actor do "trade give and take" just do not do, righteous soul of "it shares time with other, help other but also doing real love other", this is just do righteous soul living behavior.

As real living in the macro concept world of "it shares time with other, help other, but also doing real love other" is general living, not special living, righteous soul living is not special living, just rule in the cosmos law, then righteous soul living actor hear from communication righteous soul living in destination place.

Righteous soul is first righteous soul then automatically living in righteous soul living. Just small righteous soul must be shares time with, but also do help, but also do real love small righteous soul living actor".

Righteous soul living behavior is judged on right time and fixed in cosmos law

Righteous soul behavior "it shares time with other, help other, but also doing real love other", these behavior then right the time and place judge it and create of righteous soul living energy, so that cosmos law is the criteria to create righteous soul living energy creating.

So then righteous soul living actor all gone with cosmos law court, all of behavior is every moment judge and give righteous soul energy creating or decreased, calculation, so that righteous soul it does not have to hear of "think of wicked soul" rerun of past did, wicked soul make righteous soul me did creating righteous soul energy to be decreased, so "think of wicked soul' is still all "revenge and break" righteous soul me.

"Think of wicked soul" reminds me to do "revenge me and break other" truly righteous soul me did done, so that all is calculate and finished righteous soul living behavior, all decide judged by cosmos law court, righteous soul me is righteous soul living behavior of law "it shares time with other, help other, but also doing real love other", if righteous soul me so cosmos law, then defined doing righteous soul me, then all of case is end, so that truly righteous soul me, it don't necessary past finished behavior but concentration to run to the righteous soul living in destination place hurry run is major concerning thing.

But "think of wicked soul" get out past case, then make me know that "some how wicked soul me get from righteous soul behavior; all finished and calculated so then fully rewarded" but wicked soul past case end make me do get from others, this is make anger to other, so then deceit then flow "think of wicked soul" then already rewarded of creation of righteous soul living energy must be decreased result, it is "think of wicked soul" do "revenge and break" .

So that "think of wicked soul" just all depend on righteous soul behavior of residue of past righteous soul behavior is connecting push me of "think of wicked soul", please make sure righteous soul again do not deceit "thinking of wicked soul" is perfectly all is not true, "thinking of wicked soul all is related with past finished behavior" so that all is calculated, so righteous soul must do not deceit "think of wicked soul", if deceit to the "think of wicked soul" then sure of macro concept world being make other being hard, because "me" is used wicked soul of "revenge and break others", this is so foolish behavior, righteous soul living is always being "clean clear" so that nothing happened, but peace and excitement with other.

On today all of calculated judged by cosmos law court, then "think of wicked soul" issue up is all make righteous soul created righteous soul energy decreasing, so "think of wicked soul" just do "revenge and break", then if righteous soul deceit not truth follows then it is "thinking of wicked soul" then it must be get on "cloudy in micro concept world, then sure of anger expression to macro concept world other, this behavior is strong break rule of cosmos law, so then right behavior right judging from cosmos law, then righteous soul living for using running to the righteous soul living in destination place. "Thinking of wicked soul" is so cunning to make use righteous soul me, both make salver of wicked soul, but also make decreased righteous soul living energy.

"Righteous soul living behavior is judged on right time and fixed in cosmos law" this is strong righteous soul remember it, because in the micro concept world, wicked soul keep temptation to be deceit then make righteous soul me wicked soul salve to carry out "revenge and break", wicked soul do not do, but other making do "revenge and break", so then righteous soul do lose time, then soon to be capture of being wicked soul slaver.

Righteous soul can discriminate broadcasting from "thinking of wicked soul", so that righteous soul hears only broadcasting from righteous soul living in destination place.

Truly broadcasting from righteous soul hard to earing because "think of wicked soul" hearing disturbance, that very temptation past what righteous soul already calculate old case, push me, keep saying " think of wicked soul try to me detail how to do "revenge and break", this is so cunning, just very soft and what I have feeble point offending, so then righteous soul me going being temptation, then "think of wicked soul" very lower saying but give information to do "revenge and break", this is so dangerous, because if be temptation from "think of wicked soul" then wicked soul strong attack righteous soul me.

So that not to be being wicked soul salver, it must be all of clean, make nothing make all remove "remainders of before righteous soul behavior all be judged from cosmos law" so then, every moment check not be retain of reminders.

"think of wicked soul" living of past knowledge and past righteous creating behavior of sacrifice, loving, helping all is wicked soul is target to be "revenge and break", wicked soul do deceit all of wicked soul world, then strong rule is "give and take", but also to be easy living, give and take time some of surplus, that is wicked soul's criteria, but righteous souls criteria is "it shares time with other, help other, but also doing real love other", so then righteous soul behavior is righteous soul living energy to runs for the righteous soul living in destination place, but wicked soul do not know righteous soul living behavior.

Righteous soul living behavior "it shares time with other, help other, but also doing real love other" is not accept in the wicked soul, because wicked soul living macro concept world is "easy living" then to be wicked soul easy living, righteous soul living behavior is not for wicked soul living "easy living" so then, wicked soul strongly make defense righteous soul living behavior.

Righteous soul living is living based on righteous soul living behavior because righteous soul do not live as the rule of wicked soul, wicked soul for the "easy living" strong power of energy "revenge and break" is used, the righteous soul energy is "do real love other", so that righteous soul living just do "it shares time with other, help other, but also doing real love other", then righteous soul living me is target of righteous souls, so then righteous soul living is possible.

Righteous soul living growth is not to be follows "think of wicked soul" this is the rule to the righteous soul living actor, it must be already did broadcasting from righteous soul living in destination place, "do not follow, do not hearing of thinking of wicked soul" then righteous soul will safe running to the righteous soul living in destination place.

Righteous soul living growth only hearing broadcasting is creation of knowledge, truth, this is real, so then all of creation of knowledge through "micro concept -1/∞~+1/∞", must all be making "nothing", so called "righteous soul & nothing" is righteous soul living is growing.

All of remainders are being zero, 1/∞ so that every moment make clean clear micro concept world, then "the think of wicked soul" do not living even attacking righteous soul me, but "righteous soul & nothing" without remainder, then righteous soul living and growing but also keep running to the righteous soul living in destination place.

Truly wicked soul and righteous soul is keep in front line, so that righteous soul watching out "think of wicked soul" then just watch, then cosmos law also know that righteous soul is not breaking law, then keep running to the righteous soul living in destination place.

Be sure "righteous soul righteous behavior is all do calculated righteous soul living energy" so that to the righteous soul me all is settle, if "think of wicked soul" push me is all lie, deceit, do not follow it, do not hear, it, righteous soul me must do clean in the micro concept world.

Righteous soul, cosmos law

Righteous soul living grows with cosmos law. Micro cosmos law court, this is living criteria. How to live in the micro concept world is keep in a cosmos law. Righteous soul is only living by dong real love that is so weak compared with wicked soul "revenge and breaking energy" but also mind "it getting much more than other".

But righteous soul living is " it shares time with other, help other but also doing real love other", then who defense righteous soul from wicked soul, and mind, that is the "cosmos law", if do keeping righteous soul then righteous soul living energy is increased but do not keep a cosmos then righteous soul living energy is decreased.

In the living of righteous soul when is grow and down, righteous soul energy weak wicked soul energy is surge up then righteous soul be risk then righteous soul energy being decreased, this is strong power of wicked soul, this is not known to the righteous soul living actor but it must be inferring that wicked soul world also has the power surge up is possible.

Cosmos law

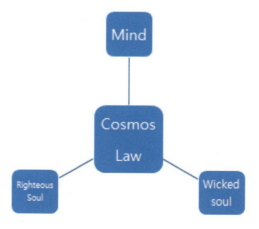

Cosmos law is only same in the macro concept world Mind, and micro concept world righteous soul, wicked soul all be adopt for the law, if keep a cosmos law then righteous soul living energy increased, but also if possible of mind keep in cosmos law then, mind living getting approaching to the righteous soul, but also wicked soul also keep a law of micro cosmos then, getting out of wicked soul to be mind and then being righteous soul living.

What I said in the book of "A book of philosophy All of world going from righteous soul "me"" then righteous soul living energy is +1, mind living energy is 0, wicked soul living energy is -1, so then, in this cosmos law adopt then, if keep a cosmos law then,

Righteous soul living energy is +1 + increasing energy, this energy is can use running to the righteous soul living in destination place also mission carry, what is mission is " meet a lover of wicked soul, then do real love lover to make righteous soul then safe returning to the righteous soul living in destination place".

But wicked soul energy -1, is if wicked soul do live in to get living in "easy living" of "revenge and break energy using" then -1 + increased wicked soul living energy, but if out of wicked soul living behavior by righteous soul mission carry out then, wicked soul to be real loved from righteous soul, then wicked soul living in keep a cosmos law then, wicked soul -1 + righteous soul energy increased, then wicked soul to be being possible of mind of energy 0, then keep do real loved from righteous soul living actor mission carry then, must be changed like

Righteous soul do real love wicked soul lover

As wicked soul keep a cosmos law with righteous soul living actor keep doing real love

Wicked soul changed into mind level living of energy 0

Righteous soul keep doing real love wicked soul of mind level energy 0

Then start wicked soul of mind level 0 + righteous soul energy increased

As keep in cosmos law of righteous soul living energy increased with righteous soul doing real love wicked soul of mind, then keep then

In the end wicked soul of mind being changed into righteous soul of energy +1

And then righteous soul living actor mission clear, then righteous soul create love of righteous soul

Then what happened to the original righteous soul so hard to create love of righteous soul, this is righteous soul create righteous soul living in micro concept $-1/\infty \sim +1/\infty$, in the micro cosmos law criteria is strong helping righteous soul living do real love wicked soul making righteous soul possible.

Micro cosmos law is righteous soul living possible, if do not have micro cosmos, then which is righteous energy increasing criteria is not but cosmos law is making possible righteous soul living survive and righteous soul living mission is possible.

As the macro concept world righteous soul living is keep a cosmos law then, it is righteous soul living behavior is "it shares time with other, help other, but also doing real love other".

Then doing righteous soul living behavior then all is secure of running to the righteous soul living in destination place living possible, micro cosmos law that wicked soul do not lie to the righteous soul wicked soul do deceit righteous soul to be misled to the righteous soul living in destination place going.

"Righteous soul, cosmos law" righteous soul and cosmos law is safe living possible in the macro concept world, then among wicked soul "revenge and breaking" mind of "getting all" all of hard living but wicked soul is "the poor & righteous soul" then righteous soul living energy is increased so that as living of righteous soul is possible.

Righteous soul living is very simple, do righteous soul living behavior "it shares time with other, help other, but also doing real love other" is keep a cosmos law coincidence so that righteous soul living behavior is real living, so that if follow of hearing broadcasting of creation of knowledge also keep in cosmos law, so that righteous soul living is keep running in the orbital in the cosmos to the righteous soul living in destination place.

Righteous soul living mission is very clear, this is save wicked soul from wicked soul living in destination living actor of "revenge and break" so that, if righteous soul living actor keep a mission clear then, in the all of macro concept world living place being living of righteous soul living destination place.

Righteous soul living in destination place is all of righteous souls are destination place is being righteous souls living place, this is righteous soul living actor until now being safe living from wicked soul, the perfect place, reaching at the righteous soul living in destination place is being real living, all overcome of hard living in the macro concept world, righteous soul living hard living who know, "the poor of righteous soul living" is so hard, this is sometimes do not eat, but also sometimes despise me, even all segregate from wicked soul and mind level living actors, how to do that, this is so hard, why righteous soul me is birth, so poor living, but the living is righteous soul living.

Endless move, this is keep cosmos law, but keep distance from wicked soul, much more than distance from mind who is all collet to be getting much more than others, how to explain," the poor & righteous soul" mind level and wicked soul said to the "the poor & righteous soul" then just beggar of lazy, but yes somehow possible, but "the poor & righteous soul" is living keep a cosmos law and learning communication from righteous soul living in destination place, so that in the micro concept $-1/\infty \sim +1/\infty$ is feel in clean clear, this is open micro and macro, so that this is true living.

In the macro concept world to be living only me, then the moment, is wicked soul easy living, mind of getting much more than others, so then wicked soul, and mind living is do not keep a cosmos law, so that wicked soul and mind do not know righteous soul living behavior of "it shares time with other, help other, and doing real love other".

But "the poor & righteous soul" do live in "it shares time with other, help other, but also doing real love others" this is real living, but also in the righteous soul living in destination place living is same living of macro concept world righteous soul living behavior of keeping in cosmos law, cosmos law is all adopt macro and micro so that micro concept world righteous soul living in destination place also adopt of micro cosmos law.

Micro cosmos law is basic law keep consistence of righteous soul living in destination place.

This is critically important in the macro concept world trained and learning is required to do, so that righteous soul living is hard in the macro concept world, because righteous soul living is voyage to the righteous soul living in destination place.

Running to the righteous soul living in destination place is so excitement, because the destination place is all of living of righteous soul living actors are all wait me safe returning to the righteous soul living in destination place.

The place is all righteous soul of creation of knowledge, all is true, there is nothing of wicked soul, nothing of mind, the place is all righteous soul, the place is trust, and help, and feeling in excitement of real living, is the living place is righteous soul living in destination place.

Righteous soul living is created, then the living is being living eternity of creation of knowledge, truth knowledge generator, so that the living is truth, not to be deceit from wicked soul, this is living of righteous soul living.

Above all living on the truth of righteous soul living, this is real living, in the macro concept world, the purpose of living is lost all is do not know where to go, all of living of wicked soul and mind is lost to go, but righteous soul me, now writing this book, righteous soul me know that which is righteous soul living, but also keep running to the righteous soul living in destination place going.

So that righteous soul me keep a cosmos law of "it shares time with other, help other but also doing real love other"

Righteous soul & wicked soul

Righteous soul & wicked soul is comes from micro concept, but truly this is micro cosmos, so that all is runs by the micro cosmos law. But righteous soul created from righteous soul living in destination place, but wicked soul is from wicked soul living in destination place, wicked soul is not created but from macro concept world to micro concept world wicked soul living in destination place.

What is this, wicked soul is from macro concept world living before after that comes to the wicked soul living in destination place, these wicked soul all did living was macro concept world, but they are all live in the way of wicked soul, so that after they returning to the wicked soul living in destination place.

But macro concept world living of righteous soul living way, in the starting created righteous soul has mission being righteous soul and as the righteous soul doing real love lover of wicked soul to make righteous soul then carry to righteous soul living in destination place, so that righteous soul is ultimate eternity living in destination place.

In the cosmos law, cosmos law is try to make all to be live in righteous soul living in destination place safe reach at then to be living in eternity living of righteous soul living; "it shares time with other, and help other, but also doing real love other' so that cosmos law is all of voyage in the cosmos then all to be being righteous soul and safe returning to the righteous soul living in destination place.

In the cosmos law is

Righteous soul created being righteous soul then save wicked soul lover of wicked soul,

In micro concept world before comes to the macro concept world, created righteous soul meets wicked soul, so then wicked soul is connected with before macro concept world, but righteous soul is created soul, so that create righteous soul voyage to be living in with body, this is all new, but wicked soul is try to "easy living" because before world is so hard living, but also after living then return to the wicked soul living in destination place.

So that wicked soul is intend to do "revenge and break" as again comes living with body, this wicked soul and new created righteous soul meet in the micro concept world, then in this principle is cosmos law, then wicked soul living has chance to live being righteous soul, because wicked soul living live with righteous soul, so that if very closed wicked soul living with righteous soul, so that righteous soul has tool to help wicked soul is " do real love", this is usual, all of righteous soul is living of "it shares time with other, help other, but also doing real love other" so that righteous soul do "real love to faced wicked soul is natural", so then this is very simple but complicate, righteous soul living is all of effort to do righteous soul living behavior is righteous soul can live survive from wicked soul, because wicked soul is "revenge and break" is all of target after that living in "easy living " wicked soul living behavior, so righteous soul is must do wicked soul energy is some of lower of "revenge and break" so that righteous soul living is survive.

Righteous soul to wicked soul is righteous soul must be role to wicked soul make righteous soul, so that in the micro concept world meet, in the souls room then, righteous soul all do righteous soul behavior, then wicked soul be excitement with righteous soul, so that wicked soul be procedures of "wicked soul -1 + strong righteous soul +1" then wicked soul is by doing real love form righteous soul = being mind living of energy 0, then keep in string righteous soul do real love "wicked soul of mind living=0, then keep doing real love in the end wicked soul mind 0 + righteous soul energy +1=wicked soul of righteous soul being", then

Micro concept world of soul room living actor is being both righteous soul, then in the living of macro concept world being living in righteous soul me, this is wicked soul living actor being disappeared, so that righteous soul me living is possible, so then, at now living in macro concept world, so strong macro concept world but also the living of macro concept world, mind level living, and wicked soul living, but also righteous soul living all of living actors are living, then righteous soul to be survive is very urgent, so that righteous soul living is "the poor & righteous soul" and keep grow then righteous soul reach at the "righteous soul and nothing" this is righteous soul living.

But to the wicked soul living is only possible with righteous soul, this is so strange wicked soul is 'revenge and break other" but righteous soul is "doing real love" is meeting in the soul room, this is living, macro concept world living is all is urgent and all of effort to living, this is survive in the macro concept world.

Here is so important wicked soul with righteous soul, righteous soul living has survive and do real love wicked soul is all is hard, but righteous soul do real love wicked soul, so then wicked soul also living in "revenge and break" but wicked soul living with righteous soul who is enlighten living in the macro concept world, so then mind $=1/\infty$, righteous soul is main behavior is "do real love wicked soul" this is both to be survive as righteous soul but also save wicked soul to create righteous soul. So then righteous soul living is how to hard, all of living is fierce living.

Righteous soul living main concerning is do real love wicked soul to create righteous soul, then righteous soul me getting better to live in the macro concept world but also righteous soul runs to the righteous soul living in destination place, in the end creative righteous soul did what expected by creator, creator expected righteous soul me to do, at first safe returning, but also do create making from wicked soul to righteous soul, so that this is righteous soul, righteous soul to wicked soul is strong closed living, so that if do fierce living righteous soul living behavior; it shares time with other, help other, but also doing real love other', then righteous soul living must be disappeared by string wicked soul, so then created righteous soul living is lived to wicked soul living.

It must be wicked soul to be real loved from righteous soul, then being righteous soul living, but also righteous soul do real love wicked soul, to create righteous soul so that both wicked soul is being end of circulation of cosmos, so then end of voyage but also, created righteous soul also all of suffering of righteous soul living behavior then, created righteous soul be grown to fully righteous soul living, so that creative righteous soul living is being real of righteous soul living of eternity living in the righteous soul living in destination place.

Righteous soul grows with n/360°

Righteous soul growth with n/360°. This is means that if n=360 then, 360/360°, in this case, it being 360° so that if reach at 360° then, the 360° angle is

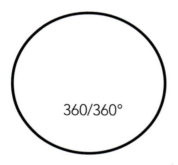

360/360°

this is n/360° then n=360, being circle..

righteous soul is growing n/360°,

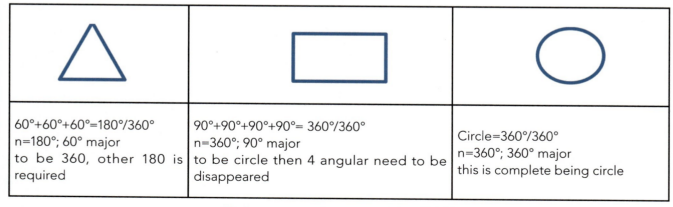

60°+60°+60°=180°/360° n=180°; 60° major to be 360, other 180 is required	90°+90°+90°+90°= 360°/360° n=360°; 90° major to be circle then 4 angular need to be disappeared	Circle=360°/360° n=360°; 360° major this is complete being circle

Righteous soul grows with n/360°

Righteous soul grows with n/360°, if n is 180° of 60° of living, this living is 60° living, 60 be being 360° it required to do time and do living in righteous soul living, truly this is half and half it must be possible to be wicked soul living, but also being righteous soul living. this living is sharp points are if this living actor running then it must be do harm others, so then this is must be compared with wicked soul energy -1.

But 90°+90°+90°+90°= 360°/360°, n=360°; 90° major then it must be accomplished of 90°×4=360°, so then it must be infer of beginning to be living in righteous soul, but in this case major is 90° so that if run this actor then hard to do harm but also getting well, so then this is compared with mind of energy 0.

Circle=360°/360° n=360°; 360° major, in this case is n/360°, then n= 360° so that if must be possible of 360°/360°= 1, this is being reach at the real living of righteous soul, so the living actor run do not harm other but make the circle running is help other 60°+60°+60°=180°/360°, n=180°; 60° major, to be making possible by the cutting by rolling circle so then infer of possible to be being 90°+90°+90°+90°= 360°/360°,n=360°; 90° major then this is being mind of energy =0, then keep Circle=360°/360° n=360°; 360° major, in this case is n/360°, then n= 360° so that if must be possible of 360°/360°= 1 make possible "90°+90°+90°+90°= 360°/360° n=360°; 90° major" to be being "Circle=360°/360° n=360°; 360° major".

Truly righteous soul living actor living is "it shares time with other, help other, but also doing real love other",

Circle of being 360°360°=1 living of righteous soul is perfect so that, circle runs meet triangle, quadrangle, then circulation runs then smash sharp points, so then being possible then, circle runs to possible run, but so that helping possible triangle, quadrangle to be circle, in the end of circle running.

So then circle is trend to runs, so then runs make possible circle move but also, triangle, quadrangle being making circle, but actually triangle, quadrangle do not help these triangle, quadrangle to be circle, so that only to circle make triangle, quadrangle to circles.

Then how to be being n/360°= 1 of righteous soul living, then n= must be reach at the 360°. N= must be being keep running to the end of 360°.

N= 1 2 3 4 5 ……360° then it must be turf to being soft, but also shallow to being deep in living is necessary. Who knows souls, mind all has option, I will not go to 360°, but I will live only n=10°, what is difference this is must be feeling in excitement degrees. What motive being living in 360° living, as beginning to end of 360° is being going so deeper, the angel is for example 3,4 is clear of seen sharp point, triangle, quadrangle so that this is macro concept world, but to be about 350° then is not seen clear but circulation shape is not circle. But to be being 360° then being clear of round, who in this reach at then being righteous soul strong +1 energy using.

Righteous soul grows with n/360°

Righteous soul living and grows to 360°, this is sure of clear of living reaching at is comes, this is by number expression to be being safe reach at righteous soul living in destination place.

Here is this is n/360° then n=360, being circle, n=360, then it comes to n/360°= formula, this is how to reach at the righteous soul living is defined so that n=360 then, it must be micro concept of "-1/∞~+1/∞" arriving,

Infer of 360°/360° is reach at righteous soul living in destination place, so then, being "righteous soul & nothing", here is being nothing, so called n=360° is reach at micro concept of "-1/∞~+1/∞", n=360 is compared with beginning 1,2,3,4,5,6,7,8,9,0, so then here is n=360=0="-1/∞~+1/∞".

Truly righteous soul grows to be being n=360/360, this is righteous soul living.

So then righteous soul living is feeling is unseen world living excitement in the macro concept world, of seen world. Ture living of excitement is not in the seen world living but unseen world living place is located at n=360, so then this is being feeling excitement of being reach at righteous soul living in destination place.

Here is in the end it conclusion that, just micro concept and righteous soul living place is truly 360/360 end, 1234567890, 0, but also micro concept -1/∞~+1/∞, so then "righteous soul & nothing", ultimate the circle, round is as reach at n=360 then, the space is being "nothing of righteous soul", in the circle living in righteous soul & nothing.

360/360°
=righteous soul
& nothing

this is n/360° then n=360, being circle.

"Righteous soul grows with n/360°", n= to be being 365, then it must be keep running to the 360, but while running to the 360, then wicked soul of triangle is make "revenge and break" but also quadrangle of mind of "getting much more than others" if righteous soul me, lose keep running then be temptation from wicked soul, and mind then, how to reach at the n=360, if do not reach at 360, then the circle, round shape is if reach at 300° then rounding shape is not exact circle, so that the shape is not harmony with righteous soul living in destination place.

If do not living in righteous soul living then wicked soul of triangle, but also mind living of quadrangle living only, just this living all not compared with round, so that the living is debt living, only round living is credit living. just in the macro concept world living righteous soul living is being enlighten but also reach at the 360=n, so that all of procedure is overcomes in the end, the living is being all living with cosmos law keeping, righteous soul living safe living then in the end of macro concept world being safe returning to the righteous soul living in destination place.

This is real living of" Righteous soul grows with n/360°"

Righteous soul helping make known creature of knowledge for running to the righteous soul living in destination place

In the living of macro concept world living place, righteous soul living actor hear of broadcasting from righteous soul living in destination place which is now macro concept world feel as "creation of knowledge, truth" this must be spread as the behavior of righteous soul living "it shares time with other, help other, but also doing real love other".

Truly righteous soul living "creature of knowledge" is in the righteous soul living actor micro concept "$-1/\infty \sim +1/\infty$" so that only lie in the micro concept is located at micro concept, truly all of living actor who is living wicked soul, mind or righteous soul has, but do not enlighten so that do now know what I have micro concept, so that if righteous soul me talk to the "do not know micro concept" then righteous soul me try to make known micro concept and through micro concept "$-1/\infty \sim +1/\infty$" this is tools to hear of broadcasting from righteous soul living destination place righteous soul behavior of "it shares time with other, help other but also doing real love other"

This is possible macro to micro, micro to macro, this possible point is micro concept "$-1/\infty \sim +1/\infty$", this is macro to micro, micro to macro connect point. So then micro concept world righteous soul do behavior to do shares macro concept world, and help macro concept world, and do real love macro concept world, vice versa.

Righteous soul me depend on micro concept world righteous soul helping me to spread righteous soul living world living way, so called macro concept world through micro concept -1/∞~+1/∞, then righteous soul me just hearing creation of knowledge to do help the ignorance of wicked soul, and mind but much more than safe living of righteous souls, on today I felt that taxi driver response is so wanted to so that it must be hard but if righteous soul me hear broadcasting from righteous soul living in destination place, pre runner who safe finished in macro concept world living finished righteous soul can help me, righteous soul me expect that.

Righteous soul living must be spread but also all of living actors in the macro concept world then macro concept world living actors will be feel excitement, because all of macro concept world living actors are losing from cosmos orbital from beginning to destination road, this is must be running to the starting point start now running, but they are all roamed out of orbital so that righteous soul me can make enlighten ignorance living actors.

Truly I'm fear, how to I do, but righteous soul me, use me to spread creation of knowledge then, righteous soul me living be fit role of righteous soul me.

Surprisingly all of living actors are all losing from orbital, all is just roamed there is no truth, so then they are all vain living who are so pity from righteous soul living in destination place.

If righteous soul living in destination place use me in the macro concept world make known to the wicked soul and mind level living actor how to Righteous soul helping make known creature of knowledge for running to the righteous soul living in destination place " so that they are also be living in running to the righteous soul living, then even they are now not righteous soul, but keep living in righteous soul living knowledge then other to be possible righteous soul living be getting energy but also open for them micro concept "=1/∞~+1/∞" this is so excitement living.

Righteous soul me hearing from righteous soul living in destination place through micro concept -1/∞~+1/∞, then now keep writing, but other method is broadcasting to macro concept world, then huge living actor will be hear of micro concept world of real living they will be known simple living "it shares time with other, help other but also doing real love other".

"Righteous soul me" do "Righteous soul helping make known creature of knowledge for running to the righteous soul living in destination place.

Creature of knowledge; creature of knowledge is truth, creation of knowledge is knowledge how to run to the righteous soul living in destination place, creation is macro concept world problems solving, this creation of knowledge is all of living has micro concept "$=1/\infty\sim+1/\infty$" this gate from macro to micro, micro to macro, so then macro will know from micro concept "$-1/\infty\sim+1/\infty$" but who find what I have micro concept "$-1/\infty\sim+1/\infty$" this is possible, all of living actor living righteous soul is possible, so that righteous soul me, share of creation of knowledge righteous soul me possible believe all is righteous soul will help me in the lecture, so then all is not me but righteous soul me using micro concept broadcasting to the macro concept world living actors.

Then they will live in righteous soul living, in the end they can live righteous soul living way, in the end they all be living in righteous soul is possible, but also righteous soul living is keep in orbital so that safe living running to the righteous soul living in destination place.

Other being living in righteous soul, then righteous soul me strong possible living in righteous soul because as increased righteous soul, then living place system is make possible righteous soul living is better than ever, so that the living is simply being of "it shares time with other, help other, but also doing real love other", so that righteous soul living actor living is being air, keep living then reach at the righteous soul living in destination place.

Righteous soul me and cosmos law

Righteous soul me living must be clear, try to be make zero of righteous soul living grounds. Righteous soul living grounds are all used by wicked soul who is use righteous soul past grounds is wicked soul living energy.

Righteous soul living grounds is make not clean clear, this is important righteous soul living growing. If righteous soul living grounds are all used up then wicked soul do not use it, the wicked soul must be decreased.

Why all of righteous soul living after has grounds? This is still righteous soul me is growing righteous soul, so that it required to me, still mixed with mind, and wicked soul living in righteous soul living.

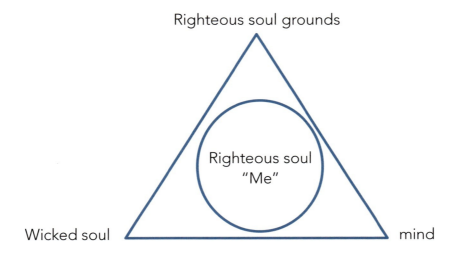

Righteous soul me try to be just circle, but at now real living is endless produce of righteous soul grounds, wicked soul keep get righteous soul grounds then keep "revenge and breaking me", righteous soul living with mind=1/∞, so that mind is trying to surviving then righteous soul must be critically dangerous.

How to be pure of righteous soul "me" circle, this is must be solution is probably "cosmos law" righteous soul living with keep a cosmos law then, there is no produce righteous soul living grounds.

"Righteous soul me" is know that cosmos law is hold true, macro concept world and micro concept world is all hold true. Here is micro concept world, so that called as micro cosmos law.

If righteous soul living, then it must be micro cosmos law will be judged then, the behavior must be setting with judge, so that some good is "righteous soul living energy increased" some worse "righteous soul living energy decreased"

Clear finished righteous soul living. Then this is must be it already past prison closing, and then it must be do not use wicked soul living energy.

Righteous soul me living growing is running to the righteous soul living in destination place.

Please righteous soul me living with variable living actors; wicked soul, righteous soul, mind level living actors.

Then righteous soul me moving then created, sometimes be attacked from wicked soul, then righteous soul must be damaged, then this is hard but it already past, but aster this attacking then created grounds, this is being cloudy make hard living of righteous soul living in clean clear.

How to do for the purpose of righteous soul living clean clear, then as possible as can send to the micro cosmos law court. Then it must be end of the wicked soul attacking me. But also do not know but wicked soul know that so that, in a moment "thinking of wicked soul brining up to me" this is strong ground, wicked soul push me do "revenge and break on ground", strangely there is no good but mostly bad" it is so strange how to making concept of strong "revenge and break", so then ignorance and wicked soul use this "think of wicked soul bring grounds"

In the micro cosmos law is clear, in the micro concept world has rule to live in righteous soul been live in clean clear, so that righteous soul me, must be helped from wicked soul attacking me, but best living is distance living with wicked soul.

Wicked soul is shown to righteous soul me is "think of wicked soul", this is micro concept world face of hard righteous soul me, but in the macro concept world, an ignorance living actor used "think of wicked soul" so then ignorance living actor do carry "thinking of wicked soul', this is so scare, macro concept world wicked soul follows of thinking of wicked soul, so that anger and revenge and break seen world scare thing are happened.

Cosmos law all count on, if wicked soul living behavior as follow of "thinking of wicked soul" then a actor wicked soul living energy is increased, but righteous soul living energy must be decreased.

Cosmos law count on that, an actor living is most follow of "thinking of wicked soul" then the living criteria is wicked soul living, then the behavior is all based on "thinking of wicked soul" the actor living world is wicked soul living, this means that cosmos law count on wicked soul living energy is increased.

It never ever "thinking of wicked soul" is not true, but all of wicked soul and minds are use "think of wicked soul' because they do not know can hearing from righteous soul living in destination place, that is righteous soul living actor hear of broadcasting.

Righteous soul living broadcasting is connect with micro concept "-1/∞~+1/∞" this is all connect macro to micro, righteous soul living actor living in the micro concept "-1/∞~+1/∞", this is so excitement getting creation of knowledge. This is possible excitement living, especially the time is when writing, then strong feeling in excitement.

So that "righteous soul me" keeps writing, writing book is real feeling excitement, but also real living of righteous soul me living possible.

"Righteous soul me" see "thinking of wicked soul' truly all of talking manuscript is "thinking of wicked soul" so then as living of righteous soul, it must be don't necessary talking, all of talking is from "thinking of wicked soul" so that talking is all ground of garbage in the macro concept world.

But righteous soul living is "righteous soul voice" there is no energy getting, the talking is from righteous soul living in destination place, then it connect with micro concept "-1/∞~+1/∞" then going with "creation of knowledge; truth" is come to "righteous soul voice" without any energy.

This is righteous soul living behavior, then macro concept world living righteous soul living is make clean clear so that the place is being real living.

Automatically righteous soul living is "it shares time with other, help other but also doing real love other' then righteous soul living place is so warm and peace living.

This is micro cosmos count on "righteous soul living energy is increased" this energy is using of running to the righteous soul living in destination place.

Righteous soul living actor runs to the righteous soul living in destination place, then this is orbital in the cosmos running voyage route. This living necessary strong energy, so that righteous soul keep doing behavior of righteous soul living. The only way is "it shares time with other, help other and doing real love other", this is just simple of righteous soul righteous soul living is creating energy.

Righteous soul living actor must be difference, just do, all of judge is cosmos law court, so all trust and depend on that, do not anger or criticize other, the other behavior is wicked soul living, then do watch, just like in the do not follow of "thinking of wicked soul', because all of wicked soul behavior of scripture is from "thinking of wicked soul', so then in the living of macro concept world, righteous soul must be do not follow the wicked soul "thinking of wicked soul of not truth living".

Righteous soul living is just living " it shares time with other, help other, but also doing real love other" then all used for that, then in the end of macro concept world then, safe reach at the righteous soul living in destination place

Righteous soul living & nothing

Righteous soul living & nothing, How righteous soul me know Righteous soul, the condition is mind=1/∞.

But righteous soul is nothing. In the living of macro concept world, Righteous soul living is not aim but just living, but also just anything another in me, truly there is no mind(mind=1/∞) there is no me(nothing), this is point of me living, but in the space is major concept then, there is no me is moving, variable living but as the mind=1/∞, and there is no me, then who recognition but the place is recognition is possible, that is righteous soul, but righteous soul is nothing, who know macro concept world me do not see me, but as the mind=1/∞, and there is no me, then righteous soul is living condition is best. In this best condition righteous soul living can growing.

Righteous soul is nothing, but here is righteous soul. Truly perfect being nothing is righteous soul living is clean clear living. in the living of macro concept world righteous soul me living is just living as the righteous soul living in the micro concept "-1/∞~+1/∞", the living is just living, there is no runs to the righteous soul living in destination place, because righteous soul living is nothing, then here is macro concept me is even righteous soul, this is just nothing of shape living.

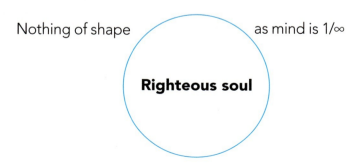

Nothing of shape   as mind is 1/∞

Righteous soul

All of shape, as the mind=1/∞ then, righteous soul is living. if mind =∞ then mind +body is=one, compact then there is no righteous soul living space is not, so that righteous soul living is almost end of living, mind is growing the early living in the macro concept world living, this is naturally mind level living but some of wicked soul living also, but most living actor, righteous soul me same feeling, "getting much more than other" this is living value, so that the living is occupied in me, so that at that time hurry living to be "getting much more than other", macro concept world time is flow, then it must be righteous soul living appeared time is comes, someone do not know the righteous soul, but in the living of macro concept world of how to living is best living? then it comes "righteous soul" this is make me real living, creative knowledge living etc.

Righteous soul living as the mind=1/∞, then this is righteous soul living.

But in the macro concept world do not living in best living, then still mind=∞, then an actor living is not appeared of righteous soul living. Then keep living mind +body= mind body, so then there is no living space. Then the chance of righteous soul living all is impossible.

All of living is righteous soul living is living or not is decide. In the macro concept world, just little living of righteous soul then, it also mind=∞, then there is no righteous soul, then the work must be end, who knows that righteous soul is remained at the vacant space, righteous soul living is all giving then the place must be living of righteous soul living.

As getting older in the macro concept world, then how to live, this is in case me also, how to live is best living is it is clear that, make best condition to live in me "righteous soul", so then it is clear of mind=1/∞, then changed mind into righteous souls, then righteous soul feeling is so excitement, because mind=1/∞, before righteous soul living in me, then mind is fake righteous soul living, so called good mind, but that is not feeling in clean clear feeling.

As mind =1/∞ then the huge space occupied by righteous soul living, then this condition of macro concept me is " I will not get my own' " I am not fear of poor living", micro concept world is 'the poor & righteous soul" and "righteous soul & nothing", this is not special, just normal living, if I living then some difference no, this is same as the living of "mind=∞", but living is real living, but also all of living is "out of mind", then "righteous soul living" is beyond of mind level living, but the living is "it shares time with other, help other, but also doing real love other".

How to do in the macro concept world, at first living purpose is changed, so that it must be known that "truth" "creation of knowledge" this is living in excitement, truly as called me as then righteous soul me seeking in excitement, this excitement is in the time of writing is huge excitement. Writing is make me righteous soul, but also being "righteous soul & nothing"

Righteous soul living is all of behavior is all righteous soul living, this is seek mind to be 1/∞, righteous soul reach at the micro concept "-1/∞~+1/∞" righteous soul to be helped form other righteous souls through micro concept "-1/∞~+1/∞" then the affairs are to be solving all of possible problems. This is righteous soul living of excitement.

So that righteous soul living is mind=1/∞, it is means that water is flows, so that righteous soul living permit righteous soul me, doing, "all of living is being itself", righteous soul me is "flow down" righteous soul living and living then, move to next time and space, because righteous soul living is runs, managed as the righteous soul living in destination place.

"Righteous soul & nothing" there is no mind=1/∞, same so then here is best of righteous soul me is possible, because there is true living, and creation of knowledge living, then very without any "righteous soul living behavior without any grounds" so that this is righteous soul of exact living. this living is being 'clean clear in me' this is so excitement with nothing of wicked soul, so called in me there is no cloudy of mind, but all is clean clear of sky.

Righteous soul & nothing is there is no deceit, then righteous soul me is living in truth.

So long "righteous soul & nothing' runs light, it must be so speed, without anything using energy, so that righteous soul living energy used for the poor of righteous soul, righteous soul of living in still growing living actor of energy used.

Righteous soul created knowledge also used at now stage of growing righteous soul can use it, so long righteous soul living behavior is related with righteous soul living all, so that righteous soul living is "water flow" water is flows all for livings, water do same as the righteous soul living behavior water is all to be absorb necessary trees and plants but also animal, other creature because with water all be living in green world, the same as the righteous soul is also do all of living.

Righteous soul living is keep supplied to do decide with breath, righteous soul living decide is driving, if just righteous soul decide and drive is doing not hear of broadcasting from righteous soul living in destination place then the decision is must be critical case out of righteous soul living, this is possible mind is getting higher then, in a moment dim of hearing broadcasting is not to be hear then, righteous soul living being same as the mind level living actor who is still keep "getting much more than others'.

Righteous soul living excitement is "creature of knowledge " righteous soul living in "clean clear" but also sure of living in real living so that "there is no righteous soul living behavior of grounds" this is do not use of wicked souls, then righteous soul living in excitement, this is so feeling excitement, all of righteous soul living energy will be used for the "the poor & righteous soul", righteous soul living actor all of energy used for it, this is how to be excitement.

But also living In righteous soul is bring all to be mind1/∞, it comes true there is no fear of poor living.

"Righteous soul living & nothing" is creation of knowledge in excitement living.

What is righteous soul?

What is righteous soul? The answer is micro concept world righteous soul living in destination place living souls.

The same as righteous soul me, in the micro cosmos law; righteous soul all know micro cosmos governing, but wicked soul and mind do not know there is cosmos law, law is adopt to macro concept world micro concept world, SEEN world Unseen world, righteous soul, wicked soul and mind in the macro concept world.

What is righteous soul?

Righteous soul living is "the poor & righteous soul" "righteous soul & nothing", but wicked soul trying to "easy living", so then it must be infer that, if righteous soul living disappeared then all automatically living in "wicked soul". Wicked soul "easy living" is "the poor & righteous soul" to "easy living" of righteous soul living disappeared.

What is righteous soul? Again ask then

Righteous soul is living in righteous soul, not to be being "wicked soul", righteous soul disappeared is two, wicked soul revenge and break energy expand wicked soul livings, then automatically, do live in easy living in the macro concept world, so that in the macro concept world living is do not choose of righteous soul of "the poor & righteous soul"

But righteous soul living in "the poor & righteous soul" who is runs orbital in cosmos still keep in road to the righteous soul living is destination place, this soul is righteous souls, just righteous soul beginning in the righteous soul living in destination place, who all of righteous souls are create then, the created righteous souls are must be living in the macro concept world, then in the place to do some role play and mission then, at now do mission carrying living actor is righteous soul.

At now mission carrying righteous soul is strong living in the macro concept world

Who is now living with wicked souls, so long righteous soul must see the living is wicked soul, so then righteous soul living actors are must be living in not "spectator" but "player" living. "spectator living is wicked soul of easy living, mind of getting much than others" these living actors are all out of play of righteous soul who is still running in the orbital to the righteous soul living in destination place, who living is "the poor & righteous soul living".

Righteous soul living is urgent keep a rule of cosmos, not to be disappeared in tour to going back for the righteous soul living in destination place, as the same righteous soul reach at the macro concept world but now runs to the micro concept world, this living is also must be safe tour safe returning to the righteous soul living in destination place.

The player of righteous soul must know to survive in the game, so then righteous soul just can live "true and creature of knowledge" this living all required to live on to know "creation of knowledge" keep hear broadcasting from righteous soul living in destination place.

What is righteous soul?

It must be righteous soul living is using create knowledge make righteous soul living time and space, so then righteous soul living is make condition of righteous soul living and also living under the suing creation of knowledge using, righteous soul living is created by righteous soul living.

Righteous soul living must do behavior "the poor & righteous soul" are hard to live in the SEEN world of macro concept world, strange wicked soul is adopt to mind levels living ways, but righteous soul living is not mixed with wicked soul and mind level living actors, so then, here is righteous soul living must do urgent and strong save "the poor & righteous souls" do keep tour for the righteous soul living in destination place, this is also role of other righteous souls, who must be ordained to help "the poor & righteous soul", micro concept world creation of righteous souls, then all of role function is given to the righteous souls, so that there is no fault in the righteous soul living in destination place, but while traveling to macro concept world then, wicked soul living of "easy living" is temptation so that, righteous soul lose righteous soul living, in the end disappeared righteous souls but living is wicked soul "easy living'.

So that righteous soul me, living place "righteous soul me" seeks a leader of righteous soul, righteous soul me want to see righteous soul living actor to be feeling in excitement, but there is no living of righteous soul living, all is wicked soul of "easy living", around of all relatives and friends are all living in wicked soul, so that there is no feeling in excitement to me.

Why now living is not excitement?

It must be helping me doing living in excitement, truly as grown then no one do care me, but this is also living, even no one survive then righteous soul me doing real living of righteous soul me, truly righteous soul me seek in the old time of righteous soul living actors who write book, so that I try to find what is righteous soul living, it must be righteous soul living must be a new and creative living, righteous soul living, and if living in righteous soul living then, personal, a just single living actor of micro concept world of righteous soul living history is required to me, but there is no, all is group and region, but personal problems solving before living righteous soul living history is not seen to me.

What is righteous soul?

This is created in the micro concept which is my first book, so the a micro concept is $-1/\infty \sim +1/\infty$, so that righteous soul is now appeared to me, righteous soul me is appeared from mind is $1/\infty$, this is hard to live because macro concept world body is all strong combined with mind, but mind is $1/\infty$ so that righteous soul is replace mind to righteous soul, so that righteous soul me is living in me, but truly only feel in writing time, righteous soul me books writing is 13 books on righteous souls, all book is righteous soul definition and living.

What is righteous soul?

Righteous soul is living only righteous soul living actor, the living solution is soluble in the every living, and strange living is all has their living soluble structure.

A wicked soul also living "easy living" so then it must be living well in the macro concept world, this is best living in the macro concept world only, so then w wicked soul use wicked soul living in destination place ordained energy is "revenge and break" so that a wicked soul problems solving is used by "revenge and break"

So long just only living of macro concept world then, this living is best living, truly most macro concept world living actors are all to be wicked soul to be "easy living" is trap, so then most macro concept world living is wicked soul living is possible.

Truly wicked soul living behavior is "easy living" suing solution of "revenge and break" then doing this way also be soluble the way of wicked soul, but this living is cosmos law keep increased wicked soul living energy, this is strong living in wicked soul living in destination place.

A righteous soul living is "it shares time with other, help other, but also doing real love other' all of problems solve by righteous soul living in destination place, so that problems solving is helped from hearing broadcasting from righteous soul living in destination place.

So long all of problems is solved from righteous soul living way, so that righteous soul living problems solving is getting energy to be used in righteous soul living, so that righteous soul safe running to the righteous soul living in destination place.

Mind living is also hard problems so that solving problems is must be wicked soul living energy using "easy living" and "getting much more than other" is most same so that mind is solved from wicked soul energy of "revenge and break energy". But also mind use righteous soul living energy, so that mind is truly living in macro concept world, so there is no relative in micro concept world, but hard to live in macro concept world of righteous soul, mind is only living in macro concept world, but righteous soul and wicked soul is living in micro concept world living.

Righteous soul living?

Do not seen to the wicked soul, and mind, jut only see righteous soul living.

Righteous soul living is now living from macro concept world to micro concept world so then righteous soul original survive in the macro concept world then running to the righteous soul living in destination place.

Righteous soul living is micro concept $-1/\infty \sim +1/\infty$, so that Righteous soul keep helping me and solving problems, so that righteous soul me living keep running to the righteous soul living in destination place.

As living reach at the righteous soul living in destination place, then righteous soul is living in eternity.

Righteous soul and excitement

Macro concept world living, as micro concept righteous soul living is keep learning living. But these days "righteous soul me" living excitement is lost. Excitement is living all, if excitement is disappeared then so hard to live on, but excitement cannot make do something, "righteous soul me" must be feeling in excitement is "it shares time with other, and help other but also doing real love other", righteous soul living behavior by products is excitement will be, to be feel in excitement is not possible in righteous soul, righteous soul me want to feel in excitement righteous soul living, without wicked soul me, mind in me all is being nothing then, whole in me righteous soul, the feeling is must be living in excitement, this is truly existed in writing, in the writing alphabet then, without writing "excitement", this is resting and runs for the new and creature living, so called that is runs to the righteous soul living in destination place.

"excitement" in my macro concept world living is feeling is all is mixed with" righteous soul + wicked soul + mind" so that something getting, some of improved and meet a human, but truly "righteous soul me" feeling in excitement is not strong. To be continued in out of unsafe but also feel in excitement is must be from micro concept world, but macro concept world to be feel in excitement is "to win in the game, so that huge living actors are all in games; online game, or off line game of favorite team game cheer up, but meeting friends and getting alcoholic beverage" "righteous soul me" losing excitement of these, then still I'm run out of righteous soul living, "body" of string difference from micro concept world living.

How I feel "righteous soul + body", this is must be end of righteous soul tour, even traveling to be returning to the righteous soul living in destination place, but truly righteous soul expected in the righteous soul living in destination place with body, then I will feel of body and righteous soul feeling in excitement. This is in the micro concept world to macro concept world living dream, but now macro concept world me is accomplished of micro concept world me being now "righteous soul me" this is peak living of excitement.

"righteous soul me is righteous soul +body" this is feeling is peak, this feeling is only writing book then I feel that, this is living on the writing time, "righteous soul me" living is true me, it must be real and true living, so that righteous soul me must be living in real living, excitement, real eating flavor, real see beautiful, real hear of sound, real smell of nose, body real feeling, this is excitement, righteous soul me must be feel and see and taste and hear of true and real and real me react, this is righteous soul me growing and excitement.

But righteous soul me living is to seek and do living as learning in the writing, but out of me all is seek and make fulfilment of excitement with "wicked soul of easy living" "mind getting much more than other of expensive premium car buying excitement" but also someone hearing artificial making out of source of excitement, these all of excitement is it never helping growing righteous soul me, but these is making do not feeling of "righteous soul me real feeling of true and real living in the macro concept world".

Just righteous soul me excitement is comes in this condition at first mind is 1/∞, so that righteous soul me is appeared up, but also as righteous soul me growing up, then wicked soul decreased, so then righteous soul living is meet body, so that being "righteous soul body" then this is itself being is so excitement, but also doing " it shares time with other, help other even much more doing real love other", further more doing mission clear of " righteous soul me save wicked soul lover out of wicked soul to be in righteous soul living", and keep living in the lover of righteous soul who a lover of righteous soul try to mission clear, so then righteous soul me lover is me, then lover do real love me, then it must be real excitement.

How to feel righteous soul me feel in "excitement" in now macro concept world me, just do is keep writing. This is only way to be feeling in excitement, so many cases be frustrated sometimes criticized from other, the other time anger to me, but righteous soul me all do forgive and do real love other, even this is so easy, but in righteous soul me in the world.

Righteous soul me inside living actors are wicked soul, and mind, all these living actors are all living of energy of past thing grounds, residue of past, so that these ground all to be used cause of wicked soul "revenge and break me" this is so fear and make me unsafe, but also invader to the righteous soul living of running to the righteous soul living in destination place, very critical urgent enemy is wicked soul of energy from "past thing grounds" all detail analysis automatically, then wicked soul push me up of analysis result, all of wicked soul result do order me to do "revenge and break" this is in the real living, all proof, if I followed analysis result then if I said scripture of wicked soul perfectly analysis "revenge and break" then other reaction is correct anger because the saying contents are all is "revenge and break", this is wicked soul using grounds are all urgent, so that righteous soul me do "burnt and water clean in me" so that righteous soul me, so fear, so that I call heavenly father please help me, but also I said that I forgive all of thinking of wicked soul, then I will send to the cosmos law court, sometimes helped god, this is righteous soul me, usual living.

Righteous soul me, how to living feeling in excitement

Excitement source is from in me, and then past grounds are all make me fear, but how to make me excitement, righteous soul living best thing is keep writing, strangely writing moment is so excitement to me, when writing then this time is living in righteous soul living, even all of wicked soul of "easy living" and "mind getting much money" living actors are do not publish righteous soul me writing, but thank "create space" helping me book making, so then fully writing, then out of stress book making, so that this is god helping me, I'm writing, it must be righteous soul me excitement is writing and writing is being book in the "create space".

Righteous soul me living in macro concept world, but strongly master is righteous soul, so that righteous soul me is master, if I feel never wicked soul then it must be feel really excitement, but it must be infer me or real me is " righteous soul; master+ wicked soul is salver and mind" then master is sleeping or losing concentration then it wicked soul try to be master positon then it must be fear, so that keep master of righteous soul, being growing righteous soul to be perfect do not related with wicked soul and mind that is righteous soul growing from the poor and righteous soul to "righteous soul & nothing" in this living is being perfect out of wicked soul and mind.

Righteous soul excitement is huge excitement, because righteous soul me is real me and true me, so that this is living out of untruth and falsehood, this living of excitement who knows, being truth and real, this is fast growing righteous soul me, just 1/∞ being in true and real living then, the righteous soul strong growing, all of wicked soul and mind trouble maker's free from time is 1/∞, then righteous soul growth strong, this is must be feeling in excitement, it must be righteous soul creator see righteous soul me growing, then creator me feeling must be excitement.

Creator feeling in excitement, then creator do give righteous soul me feedback to me, the creator mighty helping me is making righteous soul growing is so huge, this is excitement source. Creator care all attention me how to grow under the hard condition of wicked soul turbulence and mind top attacker if righteous soul me feeling "getting much more than other" then righteous soul me is disappeared from now.

So that righteous soul living is "mind 1/∞"

At now writing book is being "mind 1/∞", then feel safer because righteous soul is living, then it is feeling in excitement, if I do not feeling excitement is mind is not 1/∞, just living of mind 1/∞, then righteous soul me being in the "righteous soul & nothing", nothing is not changed but righteous soul, then it will be feeling in excitement.

"excitement" is if I feel in mind1/∞ or not, this is living in "righteous soul & nothing" but also how to make past thing grounding making 1/∞" righteous soul me feel in "clean clear" in me, this is feeling in excitement, just real see, real taste, real hearing without mind and wicked soul "thinking of wicked soul' then it must be feeling in excitement.

This is concept of "excitement" is clean clear, then all of living of excitement is defined, then only do living in excitement, because living is excitement living is running to the righteous soul living in destination place, it don't have to be temptation from wicked soul and mind, just do follow righteous soul living, this in the book, as writing then I feel in righteous soul me living in excitement.

Living in front line between righteous soul and wicked soul

Righteous soul living with wicked soul, righteous soul living do not to be wicked soul "revenge and break" so that keep watch wicked soul, it is true in the macro concept world, if righteous soul me follow the "think of wicked soul" then clear of anger as I'm saying follow wicked designed, this is true when I saying follow think of wicked soul then wife anger of my saying.

Righteous soul, wicked soul is from micro concept world; so that this is related with, righteous soul is related with righteous soul living in destination place, wicked soul is related with wicked soul living in destination place.

In the master of righteous soul must be "follow to think of wicked soul" this is righteous soul lose watching wicked soul, but wicked soul do "temptation to revenge and break" righteous soul, so that righteous soul must be awaken and not to be temptation from wicked soul.

Righteous soul me feeling that macro concept world me of body moving from to where then here also righteous soul keep watching "thinking of wicked soul" wicked soul can get wicked soul energy then, righteous soul surprisingly energy gap between wicked soul righteous soul, then righteous soul must be wait to be being energy balance.

Micro concept world

Righteous soul and wicked soul is living, so that righteous soul is influenced as the wicked soul energy fluctuation then righteous soul also to be fluctuation this most origin of micro concept world, but somehow to be influenced macro concept world, macro concept world energy of wicked soul then wicked soul energy surged up.

Righteous soul living is living then, righteous soul keep running to the righteous soul living in destination place, but if righteous soul be disappeared then wicked soul living, then wicked soul living is not master, so that it must be wicked soul living is strong fluctuation there is no harmony, so that the living must be urgent critical dangerous living.

All of time to be living in righteous soul and wicked soul, how feel tension of righteous soul living, just righteous soul living is all watch wicked soul living behavior ; all is past orientated so the past behavior grounds are all used that, so wicked soul try to be chose or to be temptation from righteous soul, then wicked soul all of effort use past acted after residue used by thinking of wicked soul, so that wicked soul do remind me to do "revenge and break" on that of residue of grounds, this is huge dangerous because macro concept world living all breaking, this is really dangerous, this is righteous soul front line with wicked soul, wicked soul so best analysis on the residue of ground, so that all of cling to the past happened thing, why the actor did do, then you must do for that, somehow mind level "trade and benefit" concept same, but this is so serious because this is righteous soul to be feel urgent, wicked soul keep "revenge and break" do temptation also righteous soul to be tumbling down, wicked soul keep series attacking.

But righteous soul living is required to living under the this hard front line, this is real living, this is the game of all time is feeling dangerous, because wicked soul keep "revenge and break", this is righteous soul is all to be paralysis, then righteous soul feel tension to watching wicked soul, but in the macro concept world, this tension to be not to be tensions so that just moment out of tension, so that all of macro concept world living actor living in dangerous, smoking and drinking alcoholic beverages, so then what happened, righteous soul to be moment being function nothing, then wicked soul living actor feel free from righteous soul watching is disappeared.

This macro concept world smoking and drinking alcoholic beverage is micro concept world is so dangerous this is righteous soul paralysis, so then this not excitement because this is feeling of wicked soul being free from righteous souls, but how to be feel excitement, that is adverse of wicked soul to be paralysis, then this is righteous soul free from wicked soul "revenge and breaking" this is must be righteous soul living best condition wicked soul is worst condition then this is music, meditation and to be lectured but also keep writing then in this pace is wicked soul is so hard, because righteous soul string watch wicked soul behavior.

Or seeing beautiful flowers, then it moment wicked soul to be paralysis, righteous soul living must be watching wicked soul, distance from wicked soul, so that righteous soul living is must be excitement because to live in body then, it must be being strong righteous soul, this is main concerning righteous soul living.

To be that righteous soul living keep hearing broadcasting from righteous soul living in destination place, the broadcasting keep deliver "creation of knowledge" this is very important to live in righteous soul living, then being survive righteous soul in the front line with wicked soul.

Adversely wicked soul also righteous soul living is strange because wicked soul living is only to be easy living all of energy of "revenge and break", but righteous soul living there is no to be getting but righteous soul living is "doing real loving" wicked soul, this is also wicked soul to be stress, because wicked soul living way is living, but strange do real love other, then wicked soul also so hard to live on.

Wicked soul living is only simple "easy living" also has the strong energy "revenge and break", but righteous soul of "doing real love" then required to do righteous soul living behavior is "it shares time with other, help other but also doing real love other" then wicked soul so hard to do, because wicked soul do not understand righteous soul behaviors.

So long righteous soul and wicked soul front line is very important region, because wicked soul living mission is "revenge and break", righteous soul living mission is "meet lover of wicked soul then do real love wicked soul then make righteous soul then bring back to the righteous soul living in destination place", so long righteous soul and wicked soul front line is all opportunity also all dangerous place. All opportunity place then all of souls mission carry out, then this is also dangerous because righteous soul to be attacked "revenge and break" so that if losing then righteous soul to be disappeared.

This is righteous soul and wicked soul front line

Macro concept world living trying to be "easy living" being wicked soul living so that, it is so hard to live in righteous soul living "it shares time with other, help other but also doing real love other", in the macro concept world normal living is closed to the wicked soul living, because wicked soul living major concerning is "easy living" do not going deeper but being easy living of wide living.

So that righteous soul mission is "find lover of wicked soul and do real love wicked soul lover to be righteous soul" is gradually hard living, in the macro concept world righteous soul living behavior so hard, because wicked soul so strong in macro concept world, but living in righteous soul must be living in mind1/∞, and the poor and righteous soul, righteous soul and nothing, but also, I will not get my own, but also I'm not fear of being poor living.

Micro concept is based all of my writing books, because out of micro concept then all is built as mixed with righteous soul, wicked soul and mind living, so that in the macro concept world, there is no find the truth but living in the micro concept world righteous soul living is possible to be truth and real living, that is righteous soul living but also, it must be possible righteous soul living broadcasting from righteous soul living in destination place.

True living of righteous soul

Truly righteous soul living in writing to me, but also in the time of meditation also, all of living is so huge front line with "think of wicked soul". Right now, my macro concept world behavior is not friend who give me time of idle talking, so that strong feeling in solitude.

This is real living. it must be not better than that, so righteous soul me living is keep solitude. Single me, this living goes with "nothing", then it must be "righteous soul me" also being "righteous soul & nothing" then it must be living me s "nothing" of time and space and with me of "righteous soul & nothing", this is truly living.

To be excitement living is created that "nothing time and space" to "righteous soul & nothing", in the macro concept world feeling is "nothing", here is "there is no mind and there is no me' so long righteous soul me excitement is "there is no excitement" because there is no me.

Why I seek being excitement? The answer is "there is no excitement because there is no me', truly all of living is "nothing" because if I be end of macro concept world being "nothing" "righteous soul & nothing", "nothing" is recognition, but the place at micro concept world living recognition is "righteous soul" but it also being "nothing", so then macro concept world all the time if I living only, but I living then keep attacking "think of wicked soul" so that automatically living is hard, this hard living is as reach at the "righteous soul & nothing" then out of hard "thinking of wicked soul", as being disappear of "thinking of wicked soul" then that is "nothing".

Why thinking of wicked soul is "revenge and breaking"?

Thinking of wicked soul role of making problem and all living of deceit, why this living going with me, every day I pray "wicked soul to be changed into righteous soul" living is just remained then drift just like dead fish, then all is end, so long just like fish keep move in the strong water, a fish to be silent water flows, that is impossible, so then as living then still produce "thinking of wicked soul", "thinking of wicked soul' is drop to the ground, if follow thinking of wicked soul then the living is being wicked soul living. cosmos law court all decision, why creator push in this jungle of wicked soul and mind and righteous soul, but I try to see righteous soul but I can't find, truly I was young I was lived with righteous soul living actors, but now I can't find righteous soul living actors.

"Thinking of wicked soul' make "righteous soul me" be hard living, "thinking of wicked soul bring fear, and stress all of hard thing bring and push me", why "thinking of wicked soul" do that, but also why my creator revealed the "thinking of wicked soul', what has programed "righteous soul me' growing.

"Righteous soul growing' is practice patience. "Solitude" "hard" "poor" "segregate" "deceit" "temptation" all of things are all righteous soul me living is hard. It must be righteous soul me living hard and good is circulation so that now living is hard state, yes, I believe that but truly now my living is hard.

All macro concept world problems is keep coming up, there is no friend, my friends also, what is living, to be feel in excitement, then use time what is this, but now my living is hard, this will be living of righteous soul living, so that I accept this living.

Righteous soul living is truly, normal living. must be all of living actors are living, that living and righteous soul me is same, even much better than me in the real living of righteous soul living why, I'm living in "righteous soul me" then try to be living righteous soul living but also these days I try to be feeling in excitement seeking, why, this is righteous soul me, truly if I do not write then, it don't have to be "righteous soul" is not come to me, but "righteous soul" is coming so that I have to live in "righteous soul'.

How hard so that last night I said that "it will comes to me excitement living" "how open excitement my god" I said it must be god has planning so that this program I will do process.

As I find "righteous soul" in the writing, so that "righteous soul me" living is fit to me, this is naturally feel in excitement, this is way of living, because my living hard but my living is in the righteous soul living, so that before writing my living has been in righteous soul living, so then as beginning writing, keyword is "righteous soul", this is fit me, so that I'm living of "righteous soul".

Righteous soul living excitement, as mind $1/\infty$, then mind fulfilment excitement is not me, but also wicked soul "easy living" that is not me, because my living is so hard but I do not use wicked soul energy of "revenge and break', just live in righteous soul living, the living is not seen, but if I runs of righteous soul living then in the end of macro concept world, then righteous soul me gone to the righteous soul living in destination place.

Righteous soul living feeling in excitement it will comes to me automatically, but now living is hard living, then some time later it will comes to me, feeling in excitement.

Wicked soul me is very excitement because of righteous soul me living in hard, but righteous soul me living is "it shares time with other, help other, but also doing real love other', so that righteous soul me also to do be helped and loved from other righteous souls.

Righteous soul me is stand up then still keep running to the righteous soul living in destination place, then in the time up then righteous soul me reach at the righteous soul living in destination place, please righteous soul me be endure then it will come righteous soul me, a excitement time will comes, today also do keep running to the righteous soul living in destination place.

Micro cosmos law

Micro cosmos law, it penalty and it blessing is comes in the macro concept world. That is clear. If living is in righteous soul living, then in the micro cosmos law acts, last weekend my team staffs worked but I did not, that is not living of righteous soul, truly weekend living feel unsafe, but I used do not work, so that my manager criticized me, but also my understaff also in his inside also, even another staffs also, then it must be my living attacking from three persons in macro concept world, but also micro concept world "micro cosmos law" act then what happened to me, it is clear the after week all of my living was not feel excitement, at first in Monday morning shower time light was off, this symptom was make known of point view of "I Ching" so that what happened this week then, all is not to be order all is out of order, truly my god is not me, instead of penalty is me, so then Thursday evening dinner time, I eat with accounting team manager then, who is invader me, then keep make me shame, so that this is also penalty, so account team manager who was used penalty for me, so I felt sorry to him, just living with me then cosmos law act.

Today morning taxi driver was so good to me, so then from now on cosmos law act be solved, it is so excitement to me, but also I met early morning hospital cleaning office building manager was seeing to me, so then god forgive me what I was out of righteous soul living.

Living in macro concept world, turning up and turning down is circulation but also, breaking a micro cosmos law then it clear penalty will comes, this is absolute true. So that do not anger of who invade me, because all is act by cosmos law, so that cosmos order is going.

This micro cosmos law is nor compensate but all is act, because righteous soul not to be forgotten if do not living in righteous soul, then the living is hard but also, if keep living then automatically strong penalty then, this is to secure righteous soul living, but to be making out of righteous soul living.

Micro cosmos, will keep "righteous soul me" if do not guilty then an actor used cosmos law actor then, who did break rule, so then who is also counted on the law of cosmos, so then the actor also been changed his behavior, this is micro cosmos law.

If micro cosmos law is broken then, an actor living out of order, then the living must be clear of wicked soul living in destination place. Cosmos law, if keep a rule then clear of giving me safe living, I feel in excitement to me, how to live is comes true, keep a cosmos law then all is secure.

Please" righteous soul me" trust of cosmos law, then you can depend on cosmos law, this is safe living in the macro concept world. Macro concept world living is so hard, this is jungle all of wicked souls and mind level living actors of a rude behavior and disrespect so huge, then how busy micro cosmos actors, in the micro concept world cosmos law is coincidence acting.

Body bread, righteous soul hearing broadcasting, wicked soul "thinking of wicked soul" but also righteous soul decision all of living is coincidence happening. This micro concept world living. so then true of result decision happened from micro cosmos law.

This living is secure of righteous soul, righteous soul will do growing all of overcoming of wicked soul rude behavior mind living of rude behavior this is how hard living, at now hard to express greeting in the morning, but that is not to be real, but all is gesture, there is no anything showing respect, the accept of courtesy is disappear, all of living is "rude behavior", this rude behavior is produce all of inside feeing is being creating "grounding, residue of wicked soul behavior source", no one knows real living of righteous soul living, righteous soul living is " it shares time with other, help other, but also doing real love other" then at first is basic sound from righteous soul living in destination place, without any energy added but the sound is energy of righteous soul transfer to the lover.

Righteous soul living of courtesy is being disappeared, this is not also in the book but also there is no museum, this living has been disappeared, so that "fragrance person" already impossible, so then human being is not to be feel in excitement, but human being is fear, all of meeting front is hard.

Heavenly father I met him, but his courtesy is not normal, but this feeling is better past, thank god, to be going well with him today also, heavenly father please help him and forgive him to live righteous soul living. Someone reading this book then, please to be feel righteous soul me, now pray wicked soul behavior of near me accounting team manager please righteous soul king make him to be living in righteous soul living.

Near me all of livings are to be living in righteous soul living then, it must be come out of behavior of "courtesy", at now in me is front wicked soul to righteous soul, near me strong wicked soul and pure of righteous soul me, so then this feeling of energy is hard to me, righteous soul king of god please help me, near man is so strong wicked soul, please all of helper of energy help me, at now some feel better.

"There is no mind, there is no me", as there is no me, then who attacking me is impossible. But actually so hard to me, near me is strong wicked soul, but this living is possible to live on, this living is all managed by wicked souls, so then wicked soul is easy living but also living is better, but wicked soul do not know, if the man is mightier, the energy must be used of righteous soul "it shares time with other, help other, but also doing real love other", then it must be feeling good to others.

Please wicked soul does not to be invader of righteous soul inner world. To be that living in "courtesy" then strong energy shares to the not strong the poor and righteous souls, if strong living actor is in wicked soul then strong power plus wicked soul energy of "revenge and breaking" is added then the living is fully "easy living".

The one way to be in "easy living" then the man styling is the man is king, but the other is not living of wicked soul living, then the wicked soul anger expression to the righteous soul, then the man will be also calculating by cosmos law, so that the cosmos law will make clear of who live in righteous soul living who is wicked soul living.

So that righteous soul living of "the poor & righteous soul" hard living but keep living in the law of cosmos, so that righteous soul living energy will be increased, in the end getting fruit. This clear, who will be getting fruit is keep in the cosmos law then, righteous soul living grow in the end of time, the righteous soul living get fruit, but also righteous soul safe returning to the righteous soul living in destination place.

Righteous soul and cosmos is a pair of living.

Righteous soul me be helped from cosmos law.

Cosmos law is safe guard to righteous soul me

There is no mind, there is no me.

Living in macro concept world, righteous soul living is variable variances are counted on that, so that cosmos law all counted on decision is the behavior is righteous soul, the other is wicked soul.

So long righteous soul runs to the righteous soul living in destination place.

The poor & righteous soul living actor also to be live in the macro concept world, by helping from micro cosmos living rule, if out of this rule then the actor living is wicked soul living, within then the actor is righteous soul living, all of behavior is all decision of cosmos law is decided.

Micro cosmos law is only doing real love other living actor of righteous soul to be helped from micro cosmos law.

Micro cosmos law is safe guard in the macro concept world, sure of it, I trust that if an actor do out of micro cosmos then, replied to the actor, I believe that this will make me safe returning to the righteous soul living in destination place.

Righteous soul & cosmos law decision

Macro concept world living, to live in righteous soul! Righteous soul living must be keeping in a law decision is required. Cosmos law is legislating and righteous soul living decision, this is righteous soul growing, going deeper is micro concept.

A act did then right there attached cosmos law court decision, then the decision is righteous soul behavior, or the behavior is wicked soul, then righteous soul me must be living ways are not simple, it must be all the time by the cosmos law, living in the world of wicked soul "revenge and break" but as the result of cosmos court decision it must be changed to righteous soul living place; it shares time with other, help other but also doing real love other.

How to be righteous soul living keep, and running to the righteous soul living in destination place, that is all of " breath, decision, act, and cosmos law decision" this is unit of living cell, all of living is connect to living cells, this is must be the behavior of cosmos law court is being "righteous soul" then this time is in the living of righteous soul living, so that righteous soul runs to the righteous soul living in destination place, but if the decision is wicked soul then the time, righteous soul running is halt, truly in the macro concept world living recognition is not guilty but in the micro concept world living is guilty is not same, so then the decision of cosmos law is correction, so that all of living behavior is righteous soul, or wicked soul is defined and decision of living.

Macro concept world living is mixed with wicked soul, righteous soul, but also mind living actors so that their understanding is correct then the macro concept world is carried, but micro concept world is not mixed with other, micro concept world is only righteous soul, but other place is wicked soul living actors so that the place living criteria is not same, but cosmos law is all effective, correct decide, micro concept world and macro concept world all same correction law.

If macro and micro concept world living actor decision is all to be wicked soul then, the living actor is wicked soul living actor but the behavior decision is righteous soul then, the living actor is righteous soul living actor, in the living macro concept world then, seen outer then which actor is righteous soul, righteous soul and mind level also do not discriminate but in the cosmos law court know that who is living in wicked soul, are living in righteous soul.

In the living is living, but the living is all judged in the cosmos law court, then all of living is all is not simple but complicate but it is very simple, creator designed "me" then righteous soul me living in origin of righteous soul living then all is simple, because the living on the orbital of road to returning to the place of created or the place of beginning, so that righteous soul me living on the orbital then this is living in the macro concept world voyage is living is so excitement, because the living is recognition of creator designed, but also righteous soul keep communication from beginning place of righteous soul living in destination place, who are care righteous soul me not out of orbital, so that in some of symptom of out of orbital then signal light comes.

If righteous soul me do not living in "it shares time with other, help other, then do real love other" then righteous soul living is forgotten, so righteous soul me living in "easy living' of wicked soul living then, as the dim of orbital then urgent righteous soul living in destination place a warning light, the case of me, then my work place has important procedure but righteous soul me, do not care of it, then I choose only me "easy living" so that Saturday and Sunday team members are all working but not me, so that truly living me was not good.

But in the end "warning signal" appeared to me, at first in the bath room light abruptly turn off, automatically at am 4 o'clock, Friday in the terminal a using bus is all disappeared all of bus route is changed, this is surprised, so then what happened to me, even this is all was partially has cause, then what is have been for 26 years using bus route is changed, so that there is no bus Monday so that I used "train", so that is not good to come work place.

As righteous soul me behavior of do not world Saturday and Sunday with team work, that is righteous soul living, so that cosmos law court judged that make me living in wicked soul, so that all of "revenge and breaking" is really act living me, this is huge hard living. usually going well living of righteous soul living, that living is keep living in righteous soul living, if not living then the living is hard living, because righteous soul living me excitement living then how many righteous souls are helping who knows.

First is around of me family do living with righteous soul me, work place do living with righteous soul me, but also micro concept world righteous creator also care and keep communication living in safe righteous soul living but also broadcasting from righteous soul living in destination place.

How dare out of righteous soul living? Who imagine that righteous soul living is real living, all of living without doing righteous soul living, all is false living. There is no living wicked soul living, and mind level living, only righteous soul living is real living, as living of real living is righteous soul living.

If do not know how to live righteous soul living?

At first must be "mind=1/∞", this is same as almost righteous soul living.

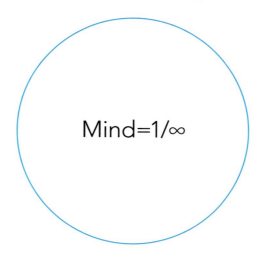

$$\text{Mind}=1/\infty$$

As mind =1/∞, righteous soul is appear in me, then called me as "righteous soul me', righteous soul me living is being living "clean clear" in the living, this is real righteous soul living, if then inside me clean clear and outside clean clear then, micro concept world clean clear, macro concept world clean clear then, the scenery is seen to me real and excitement.

As mind =1/∞, then the living is real me, real me is appeared up, so then the living is "basic sound voice" "warm feeling" automatically living in the excitement living.

Mind =1/∞, is just so moment, then moment also survive righteous soul appeared me, then this is just glance but after then the living is righteous soul living, righteous soul me, so hard living, how to I explained here I can't saying, just in me, at that time I do not know, but righteous soul was oppressed to me, I don't know, but now knowing that cosmos law court keep judged me "righteous soul' so that even wicked soul, and mind are strong oppress me, but righteous soul energy was so huge, in the and righteous soul coming out, so then righteous soul me start book writing then, while book writing I realized that righteous soul is real living, all of books are all saying righteous soul living, until now I wrote 13 books on righteous souls.

It must be all is cosmos judge me, cosmos law know that as keep energy accumulate in the end get out of it, so that being righteous soul living me possible. Cosmos law court still all of huge micro macro and all of cases are all doing judging.

Living righteous soul, righteous soul me running to now, so then, the living is not complete so that righteous soul me feel "alone" but righteous soul me, as reach at the righteous soul living in destination place, righteous soul me being excitement because there is all of living actors are all righteous soul living actors.

As I reach at the righteous soul living in destination place, righteous soul me feel in excitement, because all of them are real living actor who are not ignorance all is enlighten living actors.

I can talk with them all the day, night, about living in righteous soul, real living. righteous soul living is my really excitement source this is opportunity to me living in righteous soul living.

Truly in the book writing then I felt that I'm living in righteous soul living.

Book writing is living in righteous soul living certify.

Please create me, creator helping me living in righteous soul living, but also end of righteous soul living, safe enough returning to the righteous soul living in destination place, keep care righteous soul me.

Righteous soul living king of god, this is Jesus Christ I'm all of hear pray. Amen.

Accept it

In my macro concept world there is no excitement. Keep series affairs of me is not good for me. So then I felt that is my time, so I am accepting it. Recently my living is at a loss, so that just this living is going naturally without engine using.

My living engine is out of order, sometimes I'm complain other fault, truly my wicked soul push me to think me, other fault, sometimes law family problems, and church problems will come to me, that is not my center of living, but that is why my living engine is out of order, that is real problems.

All accept, all is not known to me, why not excitement, but also why my engine is out of order. In my work place, my job projects are all working, remodeling in building is continued so that I'm working on holidays, but also my understaffs are all tired, so that our team do not have summer vacation, so am I, my routine of summer vacation and make clean my grandmother tomb, but still I'm in busy, so that cause of it, I do not know, there is no feeling excitement, there is no dreamed. Truly I'm living in micro concept world then, my living is micro concept living, as living about 5 years then I could not have make me in macro concept of excitement.

At now I have to accept all of not running to the righteous soul living in destination place.

I'm remained at the place, there is no hearing broadcasting, and my watching "think of wicked soul" living also why I'm living this way? Complain to me, what is do me, truly all is begins that living in micro concept, so then this has been excitement, but now my living is not excitement, because my living is one them of "righteous soul" I'm keep in all of time and effort to do with "righteous soul", my book selection criteria also based on "righteous soul", so now my living is being rigid.

Yesterday was come to me "time" truly that was fully topic of writing but I could not make possible, so that topic of "time" erased but please time is why righteous soul to do me, "time" is routine indicator so that time is some of excitement of righteous soul closely related, but in me communication that stop "time".

The main problems is righteous soul me is tired, anything excitement casus of book, this is long time effort but the result is not coming, righteous soul me, must be changing time is come to me, but all of living is not writing just excitement is energy to do, I have to build in excitement, excitement is how to connect to me, even just anything "think of wicked soul', I'm rely on righteous soul living in excitement.

If righteous soul of "creation of knowledge" this is feeling in excitement. Recently I got a symptom of my living, so that I can catch that some of living is accident happened to me, for example in the early morning taxi calling then the taxi and me is go natural then the living is not changing point, but strange but there is not well do getting taxi then, the day must be not good, so this is learned that "I ching" so that I watching changing point, so now is 2 week do not excitement time.

In the "I Ching" change the streaming, so then my living is hard, there is no excitement, so then it must be "righteous soul me accept hard time" this is micro concept world living, so that this is result is accept, so now, in my family all of important behavior my daughter is examination of university, but also my son preparing getting job, but also my wife is busy nursing her father, but actually righteous soul me is free, so that righteous soul me all undertake, then this concept must be understand so that righteous soul me accept it.

Excitement, running to the righteous soul living in destination place, righteous soul growth, all of this living is also faces that hard time and hard to run to the righteous soul living in destination place, this is real living.

Oh! At now living macro concept world is hot weather also must be act, anyway now living is hard to write also. But now writing is accepting it, because there is no solution to now then all accept it, accept it, this is my living.

Oh! At now, if this saying is possible or not, please safe living with "think of wicked soul", point of me then at me is all of think of wicked soul energy power is strong, in me, there is residue of ground of real living of macro concept world, then thinking of wicked soul order me if do then, the action make hard other, think of wicked soul is residue in the macro concept world an actor behavior has the unfired residue is remained in me, all of residue is supplied to me from outer of macro concept world, here all is not digest then what is this? An actor of macro concept world living actor must be "mind level living actor" today strong thinking of wicked soul make issue up is pastor behavior of Sunday church worship then sermon contents are all advertisement but also old contents, but righteous soul me expect of righteous soul of sermon, but pester sermon has given me residue, so that "think of wicked soul" keeping pushing me, how to I do, then if follow wicked soul, then, I have to say to the pester why your sermon is most advertising then, the pester must be strong anger to me, because the pester living in pester of church minister years is 26 years, then I'm nothing to him, then how to I do, but think of wicked soul push me, to do "revenge and break", here is must be important Sunday church minister sermon must be feeling in righteous soul of hearing broadcasting from righteous soul living in destination place.

If pester hear broadcasting from righteous soul living in destination place, the it must be righteous soul do help a minister sermon, so that all of attendants are all to be listening sermon then all to be fired perfect without residue.

Today some of out of righteous soul but also, accept it, that righteous soul me, do not reject what I'm doing, because if reject at now then, the living must be living of wicked soul living, all why not "easy living" but to be righteous soul living must be "accept it".

As righteous soul me writing is for five years, but still righteous soul me just not professional writer, because writing is not influence my excitement living, so that righteous soul me living is still hard to live on. But someday it will come to me, the living of excitement.

As accept my living is sacrifice living, for the lovers sacrificing is real living and feeling in excitement, as "thinking of wicked soul" black in me, but this cloudy be moved to other place then in me is being "clean clear"

Around of me, living actors are all wicked soul living, mind living, but also righteous soul living, then the righteous soul must be helping me to live in excitement, but sorry I can't find it. Work place all of living is ranking order is used so that just all accept it, but accept it is only way to live on. Here is making energy place.

The same as righteous soul living energy getting also, it must be "accept it", then righteous soul living energy will gains.

Righteous soul living energy is getting from losing game in the macro concept world; all losing to other is also getting in the micro concept world living righteous soul living energy getting. So that "accepts it".

Even I'm "accept it" but sometimes make me excitement will occur then, it is living tools and living helping me, if I would be feeling excitement cause of book related then, this is feeling in excitement, but this is not me but readers select my books.

Truly this is real excitement to me,

But this is all god accept me or not, so that that is not as living in mind level living and wicked soul living.

This book excitement and without mind living and wicked soul living.

I will not forget micro concept is "$-1/\infty \sim +1/\infty$", I have to rely on micro concept, because micro concept is all of source of energy to write now.

In the micro concept also accept it, if excitement from book then this is all readers select this book. Then it must be excitement to me, this is also use for the living tools. The living is in the excitement then living I want to be living in righteous soul living excitement.

Righteous soul relationship with macro living actors

Righteous soul living actor living in macro concept world with body, so that it must be this is writing possible. But righteous soul living actor living in real in the macro concept world, at now, there is no see righteous soul living actor, all of meeting actors are all "easy living of wicked soul" "getting much more than other of mind living",

It must be all of livings are making better for only wicked soul living actors and mind so that there is no anything "gentleman" who is livening in righteous soul so good manners, but also do sympathize others, so then basically other is enemy.

All of philosophical concept all dried out, around of me in the macro concept world, there is no rule to consider others, this living place is jungle which is just to be good position getting, there is no " it shares time with other and help other but also doing real love other", at now I can't trust anyone .

Just one day paying taxi, taxi driver treat passenger but something strange thing "passenger superior positon behavior" so that the place disappeared service, driver and me front line was silent, this thing are all happens in the other person to person front line. There is no good manner, so that this is hell of living place, I'm declares.

Righteous soul me living in macro concept world all are wicked soul and mind level living actors in the macro concept world, so that there is no excitement in my living place.

How to living is excitement of righteous soul me, in this wicked soul and mind level living actors are all occupied.

Righteous soul me living but feeling and energy of wicked souls are huge, all of behavior is put in to me, wicked soul of macro concept world try to revenge and break me, all around of me are it never been righteous soul living. working place, family living, religious living all place, there is no see righteous soul living, all of wicked soul living, this is decide that at now living is wicked soul living in destination place.

I will not expect anyone who treats me being "it shares time with me, and helping me but also doing real loved from other" this is impossible. As I'm so tired cause of hot weather of summer, this living now is there is no vacation because my work place is so huge busy, strong political power group and my team working, they are planning changing there is no rule, all is on their ways, just like children behavior. Our team is doing accepting it then, time for this working is lengthen, so then my team and me is tired.

Who knows under the power, then just order then accept but also remodeling time is changing to be lengthening.

Righteous soul me is so tired, but this is making money living, so that righteous soul me living is possible,

Righteous soul me am right?

What I said that while I'm writing then, I have to be righteous soul, but in the real living, body temptation, body tired, but also macro concept world variance conditions that will I living in righteous soul, I'm suspicious but in the writing time me is sure "righteous soul living me", righteous soul me must to be living in "the poor & righteous soul living' so that in the macro concept world poor living is called treat me as the poor, this means that wicked soul see me, then out of wicked soul me, most wicked soul of "easy living" is watch me "the poor", but I'm an righteous soul, so that strongly watching wicked soul behavior.

Righteous soul me in the macro concept world, I feel that just one, but all is same of wicked soul and mind level, so that all of living behavior is common in the wicked soul living, but righteous soul living me is not same, righteous soul me, living is lonesome, because the living is not same with wicked soul living.

Wicked soul living actor is "easy living" not to be trouble from others, they are all best player in the wicked soul living world, so they are fighter and they are easily win, but righteous soul me living is not win, all of living is lose the game, but actually righteous soul me, living is not related with making money, so that all of interest is making money, set aside of righteous soul living.

Wicked soul and mind level living actors are all interesting with money, so then wicked soul living actor very interesting on money getting, so that huge wicked souls are living in the money transaction, but righteous soul living is not relative with money but living in the corner of long distance from wicked soul living actor living place.

Righteous soul living place is corner not a center, so that not rich but the poor, but it must be the poor must be possible to write, righteous soul living is "writing of the poor & righteous soul".

Even though my writing book is not selling but, righteous soul living only feeling excitement, this is wicked do not feeling in this excitement. Righteous soul living is just runs to the righteous soul living in destination place, so that it is not concerning from macro concept world wicked soul and mind applaud to me, that just safe living in the corner then this is feeling in excitement.

Righteous soul me living is do not make hard other, but just do living in righteous soul living, so that here is corner is do not competition to make other fallen and hard, it is not do, this is living of going deeper but wide is shorter of $1/\infty$, so then corner living, this living is "the poor & righteous soul living', depth is ∞, so then it must be calculate wide of $1/\infty \times$ depth of ∞ = must be result is macro concept world then it must be 1, but micro concept world living is 0, this is must be how to explain then changed, here is not decide which result is right, but much more important is righteous soul living is wide is $1/\infty$, so called corner living, do not make hard other.

But righteous soul living is going deeper, this must be deeper is ∞, then righteous soul living running to the righteous soul living in destination place, so that running road is going deeper, so that righteous soul living is getting "creation of knowledge" as the goes to deeper then, the place all the point is micro concept $-1/\infty \sim +1/\infty$.

Who knows in the macro concept world?

All of macro concept world wicked soul mind level living actors are all to be living of wide is ∞, depth is $1/\infty$.

So that wicked soul and mind level living actor must be conflict to others, on the land of wide, so that the place is battle field, there is no anyone of gentle man, truly if a gentle living actor it never not to be lose but all of living actors are all to be living in wicked soul of "easy living", so that wide is ∞, and depth is $1/\infty$, the living is not feeling excitement, but mind order macro concept world so that wicked soul and mind living is "easy living" but "easy living" is not easy living.

Who said that the living of wide $\infty \times$ depth $1/\infty =$ "not easy living but hard living" only. Because the wide living is all competition, but endless competition, so then, huge failure of living actors are all chose "easy living", so that in the easy living, all of wicked soul living is make jungle of "revenge and break" battle field.

If living of righteous soul living, wide $1/\infty \times$ deep $\infty =$ even this is "the poor & righteous soul" but this living there is no competition because wide is $1/\infty$, this living is all the time end of position, so that this living is being done, so that macro concept world righteous soul me living is all end positon, but now living.

The poor & righteous soul of wide $1/\infty \times$ deep $\infty =$ then, as goes then the living is excitement, but also get fruit, so that must do care of living, even first living is "easy living of wicked soul' but all of easy living actors are all condensed in a wicked soul living in destination place, who all to be living in easy living, then in the place most living actors are not in easy living.

The poor & righteous soul living wide 1/∞ ×deep ∞=

It is living of micro concept world creator expect me to do, that is righteous soul me with mind=1/∞, then righteous soul is come up, so that righteous soul me, being enlighten so that living on the creator designed.

Enlighten living of righteous soul living is keep hearing broadcasting from righteous soul living in destination place so that getting "creation of knowledge", this is real excitement living.

So that righteous soul me, mission is " righteous soul me, find wicked soul lover then do real love lover, and make righteous soul and being back to the righteous soul living in destination place", at now macro concept world righteous soul me, meet strong huge wicked soul lover, but righteous soul me, keep doing real love her, so that lover of me, getting better, it is so strange to me lover is all of nothing in "it shares time with other, help other but also doing real love other', lover is talent at as the wicked soul living, she is living well in the work place, but other is all nothing, I bring lover to the church for 3 years, then she is not interesting god relative, so that I accept of lover " I will not attend church", so that I feel ok, my wife righteous soul is so small, I feel piety her, but I'm pray for my wife, because this is mission making lover righteous soul living.

The poor & righteous soul living wide 1/∞ ×deep ∞=

At now all of livings are wicked soul, but these are all has begins that righteous soul of poor living and wicked soul of easy living, so all choose, wicked soul of easy living.

So that righteous soul living creator expect to live in "goddess of mercy" but they are all not choose of righteous soul of "goddess of mercy" but to be living in "easy living" of "the rich of wicked soul living" so that the rich of wicked soul living is originality is wicked soul, so that it never to be living in "it shares time with other, but also help other and doing real love other", this is "easy living", they want to live in keep fruit, but this is not wicked soul easy living, wicked soul easy living is not fruit living.

So that macro concept world living is not simple, how to live is decided living in righteous soul living of wicked soul living.

At now living anyone do not try to live in righteous soul living. But easy living so that macro concept world living is so hard to the righteous soul living actor.

But righteous soul must grow under the wicked soul and mind of hard living, righteous soul living must be getting runs to the much more deep place reach, so that righteous soul living excitement, is at now living in macro concept world, so that being living in righteous soul living excitement.

Righteous soul and feeling excitement

Residue of past origin comes to me as the "think of wicked soul", the real of accident was ended, but keep remained in me not real of residue, Residue remained in me so that as the dust of in me, so that with dust think of wicked soul attack me, then righteous soul try to be clean clear, but it keep arising turbulence of hard in me is produced.

This dusts are "residue of past accident", this is being "think of wicked soul" "dust in the righteous soul clean clear" "make hard in me" then feeling excitement is very tired.

At now is same feeling there is feeling in excitement.

If I see and acting with me, then a gentleman and woman but also do for me "it shares time with me, and helping me and but also doing real love me" then it will be changed, then someone in the macro concept world do for me, it must be try to do help me, then strange getting better, feeling in excitement.

Excitement and clean clear in me

If in this place then, righteous soul me there is no feeling in turbulence, this is doing not in excitement, so long feeling in excitement is source of living energy.

If my wife care me and do show me her excitement then, it is my real excitement, here is there is no any wrong, this feeling is being clean clear. Then me and wife living is very important, role player of my lover is wife, my wife lover of role player is me, excitement feeling is helped loved from macro concept world this is huge, this is must be feeling in relationship feeling.

Until now my writing is based on micro concept so that all of living writing is micro concept world, but in the macro concept world role player do for object then, how feeling in excitement, but role player do not know, then micro concept world righteous soul living be feeling in excitement macro concept world love of wife doing loving then this living make me, righteous soul, the poor of righteous soul feeling in good.

Still it is not known to me, macro concept world wife loving "me" feeling of micro concept world, only righteous soul, or both feeling of wicked soul or righteous soul, loving feeling is all accept wicked soul and righteous soul, but loving feeling is much sensitive feeling by wicked soul, so that wicked soul feeling in excitement and righteous soul feeling in excitement, then the same feeling in excitement.

This feeling excitement also complete getting, winning, or fruit, then coincidence feeling in excitement this is excitement, but righteous soul living in excitement is living in "true knowledge", righteous soul & creation of knowledge, this living is real excitement, but this feeling of excitement created as nothing of residue of clean clear in me, that time righteous soul living energy is higher, then the time excitement is real living of excitement.

Truth knowledge giving me is also righteous soul accept feeling of excitement. Righteous soul saying me "truth" then the living is excitement; this living is "the taste of living" but it must also after feeling is all to be burnt then be clear of water, then in the righteous soul living place there is no dusty, then it must be being clean clear, but wicked soul also living, so that wicked soul seek the time to be shown to me, make me using "revenge and break" this is wicked soul do, so that wicked soul has the knowledge, but righteous soul me, truly do not know wicked soul role, but cosmos, micro cosmos know that, wicked soul role player is control and front line with righteous soul, so that righteous soul must be living in urgent time is living dynamic is wicked soul role player.

Macro concept world "me" feeling" is not same, sometimes going up, the other time going down, this up and down is living itself, but in the down time just like now me, then it is righteous soul down, wicked soul is up, then righteous soul feeling urgent is so high. Then living is circulation up and down, it must be cosmos law expect because in the low time keep accept all of low time then after time of it, then originality same place going up, but in the down time righteous soul to be temptation then, in this time righteous soul to be lured from wicked soul of "easy living" then righteous soul living weak.

So then "righteous soul me" living endure of lower time, then this is program of righteous soul living in destination place. When lower time, strong of the poor & righteous soul living, then if righteous soul of high time how to use then in the lower time is doing is also considered.

Strangely righteous soul me, these days all of gone excitement so that, this period all to be endure living, heavenly father please give me excitement, righteous soul living excitement is living on the "truth of knowledge, so called creation of knowledge", righteous soul want to be hear broadcasting from righteous soul living in destination place, at that time hearing broadcasting itself is excitement.

Righteous soul real living on the creation of knowledge from righteous soul living in destination place, this is huge excitement because this is truth, if I follow this truth then righteous soul me reach at righteous soul living in destination place, furthermore cosmos law keeping and excitement.

Cosmos law is clear of righteous soul living actor secure, because cosmos law is general in the righteous soul living in destination place, so that as under the cosmos law then righteous soul living is running to the righteous soul living in destination place.

Excitement on the creation of knowledge of truth then, this living is righteous soul me being itself, then this is living by ordered as righteous soul living actor behavior without mind, and wicked soul living flowing.

Just only righteous soul living on the creation of knowledge of truth, then this is real living in excitement of righteous soul.

Righteous soul with sprit energy of righteous soul living

Righteous soul living energy is created by righteous soul behavior of "it shares time with other, help other, but also doing real love other", this is same of getting in the macro concept world body living energy getting.

So that righteous soul living energy getting is required. This is so important to righteous soul growing. This is very important concept to me, as keep writing then, creator of me, righteous soul king righteous soul god, before help me; I heard that righteous soul living energy.

What feeling in micro concept world righteous soul living energy is in the macro concept world living is this is also unseen energy, oriental living philosophy has 氣spirit energy, righteous soul living energy is require to run to the righteous soul living in destination place, micro concept world righteous soul living, then running to the righteous soul living in destination place.

So that righteous soul living energy is righteous soul living running to the righteous soul living in destination place, this is macro concept world living also same, because macro living actor with micro living, then macro concept world living actor must feel righteous soul energy, what is this, this is wicked soul is very sensitive, wicked soul is revenge and break righteous soul, but truly wicked soul do not create righteous soul living energy, so that wicked soul also to be helped from righteous soul living, so then wicked soul also feel in excitement of righteous soul living.

This case story is can be feel in the family living, an righteous soul living is keep doing "it shares time with other, help other but also doing real love other" then the family righteous soul, so called a righteous soul energy creating this energy effect family member all use energy, so that in the family living bright, feeling in excitement, so then this feeling is strong wicked soul be feel in excitement. But also the wicked soul also gradually changed into righteous soul, so that a righteous soul living behavior is make better family so that family member also to be changed into righteous soul living.

Truly all of living in the macro concept world, all has variable role play, if someone to be living in getting well make money then, the man talent at role of making money, but the other is music then the man role play is making better family, so in the micro concept world these living is righteous soul living then, it must be living of righteous soul living behavior "it shares time with other, help other and doing real love other" this is create righteous soul living energy, so then energy is circulation, this circulation of energy will be living flow, all of family members are all to be brighter living possible, that is a righteous soul living role playing.

Macro concept world living wicked soul living, mind level livings, righteous soul living, so then which is righteous soul living in not critical rule, so that it cosmos law is possible, cosmos law is all to be judged by the law of cosmos, so then macro concept world living actors are ignorance but also getting much more than others, so long, living balance so called macro concept world energy and micro concept world energy is balance is required, then macro concept world getting much more than other, and micro concept world righteous soul living energy getting is combination is required.

To be living in righteous soul is required righteous soul living energy

So that micro concept world righteous soul energy; "it shares time with other, help other, but also doing real love other"

Macro concept world getting much more than other, then coincidence then macro making money must be to be being "the poor & righteous soul" by doing righteous soul living behavior then, macro concept world living actor do live getting much more than other, but the result to be lived as the righteous soul living then, the macro concept world living "the poor & righteous soul" energy effect is seen keep living well.

Righteous soul living behavior is so huge living best way
This living by products are huge in the macro concept world living

A righteous soul living energy crating by "it shares time with other, help other, and doing real love other" then a righteous soul helped necessary living actor, then this is cosmos law court calculate me righteous soul living energy, then it is doing all, righteous soul living behavior is count on, so that righteous soul me running to the righteous soul living in destination place, is possible, but by product is macro concept world living actor keep show me "thank you", so that macro concept world living be brighter world.

Righteous soul living growing by doing righteous soul living behavior
So that to be righteous soul, then the balance is required, so then

Macro concept world living plus micro concept world righteous soul living, so then macro living is body support, micro concept world is righteous soul living support, then macro concept world is both living is required, to be then enlighten is required but from now, this book is make other creation of knowledge, if read this book then, how to live is decide.

A living actor living in righteous soul living then, macro concept world and micro concept world is coincidence of balance living. So that the living in the macro concept world being righteous soul living and real living is possible, just body living in the macro concept world, but also righteous soul living support, of righteous soul living behavior " it shares time with other, help other, but also doing real love other' is required to live on.

But also this living is righteous soul being strong and safe living running to the righteous soul living in destination place reaching at.

Righteous soul with sprit energy of righteous soul living must remember righteous soul me, be live in "the poor & righteous soul" this is balance living macro concept world and micro concept world living so then righteous soul growth to be strong righteous soul, this soul sure of safe running to the righteous soul living in destination place, in the end returning to the righteous soul living in destination do safe coming back from macro concept world voyage.

Righteous soul under the macro concept world rudeness

It rains in the morning. This rain cause of typhoon, so that I used taxi. It is so good for me, so that originality of taxi make possible to reach at my work place. But rainy day I expect to come to apt gate, but the taxi wait me out of gate, so that I wet cause of rains, just in me wicked soul anger why that driver do not come to me making not wet rains. Today morning my chief of department arrived after me, then I expect his "good morning" but his saying "nothing", so that righteous soul wicked soul estimate his wicked soul, "he will anger to me", so that keep increased "residue of happening".

Micro concept world righteous soul and micro concept world wicked soul world is difference, this is infer that in the micro concept world living actor, it must be righteous soul try to live in "the poor & righteous soul" "righteous soul & nothing", but wicked soul keep collect to all of "residue of acts" so that wicked soul keep supplied "thinking of wicked soul" truly "thinking of wicked soul" is not living in righteous soul living, because righteous soul living is based on "the poor & righteous soul", "righteous soul & nothing", so that cosmos law the feeling if "righteous soul me" feeling is all is dust living.

Righteous soul living try to be cleaning of "righteous soul & nothing" but wicked soul all collect residue so that the place is all of dirty dust useless waste old knowledge, this is used to "revenge and break" this is also make hard righteous soul growing, so that righteous soul keep cleaning dust from wicked soul "thinking of wicked soul" so that wicked soul express of "thinking of wicked soul" making hard, this is to the righteous soul all watching "thinking of wicked soul" but it appeared to righteous soul, then forgive and cleaning repeat just do.

In the macro concept world include me all of living actor in the front line, there is no criteria to live, because of personalist behavior so that in the front line living actor all to be feel wicked soul anger, so that it is also wicked soul collect this happening useless old information to be after "revenge and break" because wicked soul can't now anger expression, then in this time righteous soul will see it, righteous soul feel sympathy of macro concept world rude behavior.

Righteous soul do not collect like wicked soul, because righteous soul is supply of "creation of knowledge; truth" sot that it don't necessary, but wicked soul do not have function like righteous soul of "creation of knowledge; truth" so that wicked soul keep collecting all of happened at the macro concept world front line residue.

Righteous soul living with wicked soul, righteous soul do righteous soul living behavior of "it shares time with other, help other, but also doing real love other", then infer that wicked soul possible know of useless old reside collecting will be decreased,

Wicked soul to be righteous soul is infer of possible by righteous soul endless doing real love wicked soul then the wicked soul to be living in righteous soul living.

In the cosmos law world me feeling in excitement is wicked soul living feeling, because that what is filled and satisfaction then, excitement is wicked soul living, so called getting house, mind excitement, and wicked soul excitement, win the game also wicked soul and mind excitement, but righteous soul excitement is "clean clear of righteous soul living time and space", this is not related with getting and winning, so that righteous soul living is meet other righteous soul then other righteous soul do righteous soul living behavior "a righteous soul shared with me, and helped me, but also doing real love me" this is really feel in excitement.

But now rare case to me, righteous soul me excitement is my wife will to me, if my wife do for me in the macro concept world then it is huge feeling in excitement, this is righteous soul doing real love expression, but if not there is no feeling in excitement.

Lover role player do not love me, then the lover role player must be collecting useless old knowledge, because lover is not righteous soul, if lover is righteous soul, then all of getting to be throw away. But wicked soul lover cause of all dust, so that lover role player wicked soul is strong so that lover of role player do not do love, so that wicked soul lover of loving actor must be keep living ignorance of lover, how the lover is important but wicked soul lover living with lover is all the time is "revenge and break" living so then how hard but there is no excitement living lover to lover.

Righteous soul living with rude living actor

Rude living actor is wicked soul living governing actor, so that the living time and space is not same, even in the same macro concept world but wicked soul living collecting all of reside of old behavior in the front line, the front line is "righteous soul to righteous soul" "wicked soul to wicked soul" "mind to mind" this is segregate living in the macro concept world, but mixed then the living of righteous soul living is hard with "sympathy".

Macro concept world living is

Just like that to the righteous soul living actor then all is drama all of role players are enemy living, fighter living, getting much more than other living, there is no "it shares time with other, help other but also doing real love other", I do not know, it is strange to me, why drama writer do anger, fighting deceit, even other damage, so that this is the hell of wicked soul living time and space, why this wicked soul living in destination place living is used for the drama I don't know, it is huge scare for me, how play writer writing scare wicked soul behavior, this is really sympathy writer, the writer must be mind level living actor only to get make money so that drama play there is no any righteous soul living behavior "it shares time with other, help other and doing real love other".

Macro concept world drama

I will not use the word wicked soul living place used terms I will not use in here, because righteous soul living me is "there is no mind, there is no me, mind=1/∞, the poor & righteous soul" "righteous soul & nothing" this is to live in righteous soul living in destination place.

"There is no mind, there is no me" this is there is no mind, then out of mind level living, so then in the mind living place there is no me, after that cosmos law me is appeared in the righteous soul living me, so that it possible there is no me.

Mind level living place key word is "getting much more than other" this is macro concept world mind with body living, so that this is all of macro concept world time is used, mind living is busy and busy so that, they all used slaver of mind, they do not know the living in the macro concept world, so that they do not know, micro concept world of righteous soul and wicked soul, so that mind and body is all, so they are all fear of being end of body, but righteous soul do not fear because righteous soul living me is running to the righteous soul living in destination place safe returning is living, in the cosmos law in me of righteous soul living me is not end but safe returning to the righteous soul living in destination place, there living is eternity living.

Mins level living is only living in macro concept world, so that in the cosmos law the macro concept world is only living is beginning to end, this is not circulation living, this is not circulation living is not nature so that macro concept world living only recognition living is not right, in the cosmos law world all is circulation,, so then circulation of macro to micro, micro to macro is natural, the same as macro concept world living true living then it is true circulation under the cosmos law, then in the cosmos law then, after living in macro concept world, the living is righteous soul living of "it shares time with other, help other, but also dong real love other" then the living automatically safe returning to the righteous soul living in destination place, but macro concept world do live in "getting much more than other of mind living" and "easy living doing with revenge and breaking living" is all to be living at micro concept world wicked soul living in destination place living.

Cosmos law world is all to be circulation

Because cosmos is living, so that living cosmos law is all to be move and circulation, this is huge power of energy, so that all of living actor under the cosmos law, this is circulation, then macro to micro, micro to macro, so this is law of cosmos, all of living in the macro concept world living, this is like "force of gravity", so that macro concept world living connect to micro concept world.

Macro concept world is mixed living righteous soul, wicked soul and mind, but micro concept world is separated righteous soul from wicked soul, so that macro concept world living is righteous soul living lived or wicked soul live automatically runs to the destination place.

This is natural circulation of cosmos law, so that it never whose do not refuse, cosmos law rule, so that why macro concept world living is keep a rule of cosmos law, and keep living in righteous soul living "it shares time with other, help other but also doing real love other" is select for destination to the righteous soul living in destination place. But living in easy living with strong "revenge and breaking" then the living of destination place is to be real of wicked soul living in destination place, so that wicked soul behavior is rude, make hard others, do not know good manners. This is same as mind who is keep getting much more than other, so that to get is all of time consuming for it. Then the living is jut live ignorance with body, do not know micro concept world living.

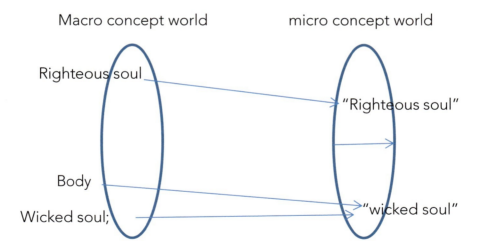

Macro concept world living is free living, but if an actor living choose to be living in righteous soul living of "mind=1/∞, and living in righteous soul; it shares time with other, help other, but also doing real love other" then this is living at the righteous souls are living place, righteous soul living in destination place, this is true because souls are very pure of souls, so that all of souls of righteous soul living at the righteous soul living, because they are lived in the macro concept world so that righteous soul living; it shares time with other, help other and dong real love other is normal living so that in the righteous soul living in destination place living in destination place correct, this is accept by cosmos law.

But in the macro concept world living had lived

Mind living of getting much more than others, so that all of time consumed, they do not know micro concept world but also, they are all busy so that they do not lived "it shares time with other, help other, but also doing real love other" so that mind level living actors do not know living in righteous soul living in destination living actors so that automatically wicked soul living in destination place arrival.

Strong easy living in the macro concept world

This is automatically living at micro concept world living wicked soul living in destination place, in the cosmos law then, wicked soul living actors are all to be living of string righteous soul living, so that righteous soul living creator expect save in the macro concept world wicked soul to righteous souls but also mind to righteous souls, but this soul is choose "easy living in the macro concept world" because easy living in the macro concept world brilliant living actor to be used as the righteous soul living, the brilliant is not use for him/her but the brilliant use for righteous soul living actors, but they are all used for only living "easy living", so that the role player do not role of righteous soul, so that the place being all to be living in wicked soul living place.

Truly macro concept world living place are brilliants of wicked soul livings are occupied it.

So that possibly brilliant righteous soul living is changed into brilliants wicked soul living, so that the place all living is hard, just weak of living cosmos, then who lead them, they are all brilliants living actors, truly in the cosmos law, the best brilliants to be assigned brining a weak souls, the same as brilliants role is must be "it shares time with other, help other, but also doing real love other", but brilliants living actor is only for him and her living so that disappeared all of righteous soul living of righteous soul living actors, then automatically all of brilliants wicked soul so that in the righteous soul road is not seen, so that righteous soul communication control center lose a best actor, the place to be living of brilliants righteous soul do not role so that, the place is being dried desert living, there is no helper, there is no share with me, there is no doing real love me. The worst living place is wicked soul living leaded living region; so that brilliants easy living "wicked soul" the first reaches at the wicked soul living in destination place.

Brilliants wicked soul who estimated as righteous soul living brilliants, the wicked soul will be very sensitive how he had lived in the macro concept world. The wicked soul repent had lived in wicked soul.

Brilliants living in macro concept world please see this book, then how to live is real living is seen to brilliants living actor. Please brilliants live for righteous soul living so that huge mind and wicked soul save making righteous souls, this is real living, the place to be living in excitement living, but also after living in the macro concept world then, the righteous soul brilliants living actor to be living in the righteous soul living in destination place eternity living.

"Righteous soul under the macro concept world rudeness "this problems all to be soluble by the brilliants righteous soul living region, because brilliants righteous soul to be role of sun, all of mind and wicked soul fully do real loved from brilliants righteous soul, then huge wicked soul, and mind to be saved and can be living righteous soul in the end all of righteous soul safe returning to the righteous soul living in destination place.

The macro concept world place there is no rude living actors because strong respect brilliants righteous soul living actor living same time, this living all to be feeling in excitement, this is righteous soul living in destination gift to macro concept world living me, this is real living in excitement.

Righteous soul with cosmos law

Righteous soul with cosmos law, righteous soul living in the cosmos law, cosmos law is all governing macro concept world and micro concept world, but also mind level living in macro concept world, micro concept world righteous soul and wicked soul.

Cosmos law is keeping flowing. This must be all infer knowing, proof is "I Ching divination" saying that all of living or not influence by the cosmos law. I Ching divination saying that some story is now cosmos law influence saying,

Just all of living is automatically going, there is no any difference, just correct moving. So then macro concept world righteous soul me don't worry some of wrong cosmos law adopt. Cosmos law is itself going, but macro concept world mind, and wicked soul do not know, because their ignorance, strange ignorance mind and wicked soul do not know cosmos law existence or not, so that living is cross the cosmos law, so that cosmos law judged that penalty.

Cosmos law is governing all of creature, there governing is all of time, 24 hours governing. So that the law is correct to live on, so that righteous soul living is surviving, if there is no cosmos law court judging then, wicked soul and mind is strong they all connecting to destroy what they want to get, then there is no living wicked souls but if just so little out of cosmos law then in the place judged and count on the judged living actor righteous soul living energy increased or decreased, so that as the all of righteous soul living energy runs out then, what happened in the point of righteous soul, then righteous soul is bankruptcy so that, there is no righteous soul, but instead of righteous soul living in me, all occupied by wicked soul, so then wicked soul living energy will increased, wicked soul living energy is used as "revenge and break" so that wicked soul me is being changed into "revenge and break" living of wicked soul.

Cosmos law court is keep flow, it never stop the function, this is make known to us, micro cosmos in me, that as the keep in cosmos law then it comes micro concept world has power to lead clean clear, cosmos law is "it shares time with other, help other, but also doing real love other", this is righteous soul living behavior so then simply righteous soul do this behavior, then why do not do behavior is in the macro concept world me is living " mind getting much more than other" "wicked soul easy living", then righteous soul living is " it shares time with other, help other, and do real love other" it is not same living mind, wicked soul and righteous soul, so that righteous soul living actor to do, in the righteous soul living, "it required wicked soul to be 1/∞, and mind to be 1/∞" so that righteous soul living behavior is fitting cosmos law, so that righteous soul living is excitement, but also the living is create knowledge, so called truth living, it is not to be deceit living, this is real living, but also this living is circulation living macro to micro and micro to macro.

Cosmos law is influenced both macro concept world and micro concept world, so that cosmos law already know that existence macro and micro concept world, this truth is only know righteous soul, so that righteous soul living is try to keep a cosmos law, and living in the macro concept world living law, both law is must be kept.

This is road to the righteous soul living in destination place reaching is not to be used obstacles so that keep a law is urgent living.

This is much more than mind getting much more than other, but also wicked soul easy living, because of righteous soul living is circulation so that not to be broken circulation so that righteous soul living is runs to the righteous soul living in destination place, righteous soul living must be "cause and effect" if keep living in cause of righteous soul behavior then cosmos law must be judged as increasing righteous soul energy.

So that righteous soul behavior is righteous soul living is keep strong awaken so that in the time of wicked soul and mind is being 1/∞, then do righteous soul living behavior. Cosmos law living is righteous soul living, but wicked soul and mind living is not cosmos law, this is general the poor living actor is lied at the street road, then mind has not time to care the poor, but also wicked soul to be easy living, there is no care of the poor, but only righteous soul helped to get out of hunger then, in the cosmos law is at first the poor of hunger living actor save is cosmos law, this is natural living also, but mind and wicked soul do not do anything of basic living, this is urgent or this is so huge concerning living in the cosmos law, but in the macro concept world living is doing not do because the lying the poor is not me but public system, so then there is no responsibility this is "easy living" of wicked soul living.

It is happened in the macro concept world, cosmos law is not kept, this is really serious result, strong keep a law then, a righteous soul living can be living in care by cosmos law, cosmos law also has the huge righteous soul energy is saving urgent living actor and the poor living saving also, if mind and wicked soul know that it may be they are all to save and feed the poor, but no one saying in the mind and wicked soul living actors so that they do live getting much more than other also easy living.

Cosmos law with righteous soul living is making growing.

Who knows that cosmos law influence all of macro and micro concept world living actors, so that this means that do not to cross over the cosmos law, then all of living to be judged then righteous soul living energy is increased and decreased is being circulation, so that righteous soul living actor keep a cosmos law so that righteous soul to be helped from cosmos law so safe growing from mind getting much more than other, wicked soul easy living, so macro concept world me living is in righteous soul living.

Under the cosmos law then righteous soul living actor living strong growing, so then even the poor & righteous soul, but in the end reach at the "righteous soul & nothing".

Righteous soul sees macro and micro me

Righteous soul sees me of macro and micro. Truly recognition is only body with living in macro concept world me secure, this is righteous soul me all see detail me. These "righteous soul" see is camera lens, this camera record me my real living all, but also this camera broadcasting live to righteous souls.

Seeing me is all of body shot so then, this is righteous soul is living with macro concept world body in, so then righteous soul is excitement with me, righteous soul is living in the righteous soul living in destination place is eternity living.

How to live after living in the righteous soul living in destination place, it must be eternity living of righteous soul will be excitement of what had lived in the macro concept world of righteous soul living behavior of energy" it shares time with other, help other but also doing real love other, this all was recorded so that this is excitement living.

Righteous soul living is all see me micro and macro, so that righteous soul see is just like cosmos law court proof all has, just see all of recorded, so that righteous soul strong power of being judged, it always righteous soul see me, and record it, righteous soul watching in micro concept world, then this is all righteous soul function, righteous soul see all of wicked soul behavior, so that in the righteous soul seeing is all of record living, here is macro and micro is all of scenery of macro concept world seen or behavior but also in the micro concept world all of "thinking of wicked soul' and "righteous soul hearing broadcasting from righteous soul living in destination place".

Righteous soul is keep watching me all of detail, so then righteous soul be sympathy of out of space orbit. Then righteous soul me is piety me, but also keep broadcasting warning signal, so that righteous soul me keep in space orbit.

Macro concept world living place all of livings are difference living, wicked soul living, mind living, righteous soul living.

In the young and string physical time, their living is free, out of rule, then it must be mercy of righteous soul living, but these macro concept world youth safe retuning to the righteous soul orbit, but most lost righteous soul living going back to the start point, of orbit forgotten.

How hard righteous soul me, righteous soul watch me micro and macro, then if macro concept me living is dangerous cross line of turning back "space orbit" out or in, then how worry it is, how to help save out of space orbit, this is righteous soul watching is piety.

Living now

Mind level living of behavior and wicked soul living is "there is mind, there is me" so that "me is "priority me" living, so that "me is much more important than others", so long this is all of living criteria is "me", at now all of living in macro concept world include of my wife and son and daughter all there are "me is priority", so that they are all living in mind and wicked soul living.

At now writing this book so that righteous soul me is "there is no mind, there is no me" so then righteous soul me is "priority others", this is righteous soul living in behavior "it shares time with other, help other and doing real love other".

Righteous soul me living is "there is no mind, there is no me" this means that righteous soul me is not in the mind level living and wicked soul living, righteous soul living in the righteous soul living, this living is "the poor& righteous soul" as being deeper then it must living in the "righteous soul & nothing", this is living.

This living "priority other" only righteous soul me, living in safe, righteous soul living is in voyage macro to micro, but also going deeper then micro concept world righteous soul living in destination via macro concept world to safe returning to the righteous soul living in destination place.

Righteous soul me is now traveling voyage, so that just watching excitement, in the macro concept world huge variable living actors are living variable wicked soul, mind, this living is not seen in the micro concept world righteous soul living in destination place, so that experiment of wicked soul living in the micro concept world, because macro concept world is all of variable living actor living opportunity living, if living in macro concept world righteous soul living then, whoever living all to be possible to safe returning to the micro concept world righteous soul living in destination place.

Righteous soul living in destination place is possible living in righteous soul living behavior this is very simple, "it shares time with other, help other, doing real lover other" than macro concept world living actor all to be safe living in righteous soul living in destination place.

Macro concept world is all are busy for "priority me" living, all is shouting for living in "easy living" righteous soul me living is just like jungle living place, all of living ways are huge variable, somehow varies but all are living is "priority me" this big against righteous soul living "it shared time with other" first action is all reject, so that all is now being closed, all of living is only one living,

Most living in macro concept world are all to be closed each living, so that they do not know righteous soul living " it shares time with other, help other, and doing real love other', this is just living with other then, it is not easy, but the living is righteous soul living, because that is not easy living.

So that righteous soul living is role of master, and another expression is role of doing honors.

This living is all of design and prepare and diligence living, but wicked soul, mind level living actors are all to be living in "easy living' and "getting much more than others" then, all is expect other for making their living "easy living" so then, they do not to be living of master living, so that they do not know master role, but now a living place, it never been possible, just coming new generation all to be living in "easy living", they do not express excitement showing to other, any place in the elevator space all see smart phone, so that anyplace doing not living of a simple of righteous soul living.

So that mind level, wicked soul living criteria all "easy living" so that these living actor and communicate and righteous soul living behavior "it shares time with other, help other but also doing real love other" is nothing.

This is living of urgent, all of living actor are worry being living poor, all of living actors living is to be rich, so that all is not matter, here is me then I'm in the hell living, so that righteous soul me living is " there is no mind and there is no me", this is real me.

Truly my living is micro concept world, just little time out of macro concept world, seen to me is huge dangerous living in the point of righteous soul living, this living is piety, if seek easy living then, adversely it will come to the "hard living is awaken", so that just like righteous soul "the poor& righteous soul" then righteous soul living is all to be helped from other righteous soul, so that just like wicked souls all of difference because righteous soul me,. Living is going with other helping and doing real love this is never hard.

All of living is not easy living then, " it shares time with other, help other and doing real love other" then, all are not easy living but this living is deeper living, so that this living is excitement living.

"Righteous soul sees macro and micro me" righteous soul living is see all of various livings, so then, righteous soul living is keep in orbit to righteous soul living in destination place.

Righteous soul living is voyage in the macro concept world, this voyage is to the micro concept world righteous soul living in destination place, this is real living.

Micro concept with righteous soul

Recently my living is broken, righteous soul is creating as mind=1/∞. Mind=1/∞ is all of my living. how hard to me living in this world, so then too hard to that, moment comes to me mind=1/∞, that it comes to me righteous soul. My living hard to me, but all overcome by own living, during hard to me, then when I was feeling is hard to breath, cause of deep hard to me, so that I needed to me exodus, then just one day comes to me the word, micro concept, so then, I try to draw in computer to be reach at micro concept, but I failed, keep deep in me, then one day hit my back head that is soon comes that hurry draw

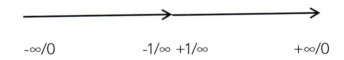

$$-\infty/0 \qquad -1/\infty \ +1/\infty \qquad +\infty/0$$

micro concept is -1/∞~+1/∞, this is micro concept, this lead me to micro concept world, that is my book writing beginning, from that I write micro concept, to now 13 book writing.

Micro concept is until now real living, and righteous soul living, but these days my living was so disturb me, because righteous soul me living but my living is all to be not excitement, there is no dream, there is no future.

But now living is hold righteous soul, righteous soul living, this living in the micro concept -1/∞~+1/∞, living in righteous soul, it is excitement to me just living routine on today morning, I read the dictionary and bible and Diamon stura, this is did today morning.

As I'm fear of poor endure of single living, so that in the board housing living is based on fear, if live in family home then my living is not fear, also do not sleep easily, so that in the board house my living is not calm every night, so that it must be single in me so fear, basically I'm fear living character, because my ear is so small, then this is symptom of living is not longer, but also it must be living in the macro concept world also all to be late, ranking in all end in the turning.

This is automatically my living in "micro concept" also why this comes to me, because "macro concept world: is so huge but also, macro concept world is mixed with wicked soul and righteous soul, and mind, truly this is living, even that is confused living, this is jungle, so that righteous soul me, macro concept world living is not major all the time to be living end, but also not center but edge from center living, so that it must be comes to me "micro concept", truly these day I'm so tired in macro concept world, but also there is no feeing in excitement, there is no any signal to me cause of book writing. So that what I have been writing is all nothing? What I have done is all what?, this is also same, so but now I'm just doing write, but it must be fortune I can express in USA, underground book making that is only express to me, so that I'm now writing.

Truly I'm not excitement, this is just so hard to me, but runs to the righteous soul living, because what I can do this only, even no one know me, just keep writing "righteous soul" this is holding to me, but also this is best to me, as that keep saying "righteous soul", as now change summer to fall season, so that weather temperature is gradually going down, it also burden to me, changing temperature is so sensitive to me, this living is hard to me also.

"Micro concept" is enter to write and during micro concept I found the "righteous soul", so then this is must be excitement, all macro concept world excitement all go down, but living in micro concept world living, so that my living is called as real living, so all of fear and do not excitement with macro concept world.

Micro concept and righteous soul, is truly not matter this are cause of me being feeling in excitement, but this is "micro concept" and "righteous soul" is whole of my living all going with "micro concept" and "righteous soul".

Truly there is no excitement to me, so that how to feel in excitement, then bird excitement is fly to the sly, fish excitement is swim in the water, but now macro concept world me is what is excitement, truly there is no excitement, when comes to me excitement, it must be just who read my book then the living is excitement then this is huge excitement, but now righteous soul me living in not in excitement.

Without excitement how to live, this is must be living in hard so that I believe that all of living is turning point, even so hard then, top hard then turning to easy living, so then, it must be changing to easy living, the moment is excitement, so that my books are all living in eternity, because these books are all writing by hearing broadcasting from righteous soul living in destination place.

I believe that hearing broadcasting from righteous soul is "creation of knowledge, truth" so that my written book is all to be "creation of knowledge, truth" this is living in eternity, so then now my doing not excitement but in the end the books are all living in eternity.

What is my excitement, even there is no excitement then to survive in this macro concept world living, then it must need to me excitement, this is necessary to me, how to live is excitement if comes to me "do lecture" then it must be real excitement, this also it must so shame and fear of what I'm doing, but if god permit me doing lecture then, it must be god helping me, just to day all to "creation of knowledge and true saying" this is not me but god, then if god used me then righteous soul me feeling in excitement.

Righteous soul me is living in running to the righteous soul living in destination place, it must be this living is also excitement, do not lost road to righteous soul living in destination place, so then this is real living to me, that is why I'm feeling in excitement to me.

Even hard but my living is voyage as the righteous soul living, and then it must be feeling in excitement because I can safe return to righteous soul living in destination place.

Righteous soul me writing "righteous soul" through micro concept, this is huge gift from righteous soul living in destination place, all is applaud to me safe returning to righteous soul living in destination place, this is so huge excitement.

As coming fall season righteous soul me, must be feeling in excitement of creation of knowledge from other righteous soul living actor writing book to me meet in a book store then, I will buy then read it, this is must be excitement, please god help me to find the real living in excitement.

Seong ju choi, this is me in the macro concept world, but I ha nick name called by myself only, because no one know me living in micro concept world, so that righteous soul me micro concept world name is "monk water". So then monk water living is just run just help living all of creature, just living as water in the all of water voyage then, in the place there is no feeling in excitement, but the living moment there is creature of living actors, so long living with me is itself is living creature of living.

"Monk water" is living in excitement at now "monk water" is so excitement it is strange this name is good to me, "monk water" "monk water" this is real excitement, this is righteous soul did gift righteous soul me, so then it must be "micro concept" "righteous soul" and "monk water" is making me excitement source, from today "monk water" so strong effect to me, because "monk water" is righteous soul me.

"Monk water" righteous soul me runs to the righteous soul living in destination place, which is the destination is not same but the destination place all same. Living in righteous soul living is so excitement. This monk water now full to living me, this is "sacrifice living" is bottomed so that living in righteous soul living is itself is excitement.

Monk water righteous soul me is feeling in excitement, but also this is so natural to me, best fit me, just small ear, small mouth, small nose, so then how to write book, this is impossible, so then I'm living in "micro concept" so that book writing is "the poor & righteous soul" this is real me, this is strong than others of wicked soul and mind living actors who are huge knowledge power, they are all macro concept world easy living position, so that the monk of righteous soul living me writing is "the poor & righteous soul" this is righteous soul me living, just one day book " the poor & righteous soul" then righteous soul me reject to writing "the poor" key word but now so lucky because no one treat a book with keyword of "the poor", it must be the poor all of righteous souls are watching me now writing, the righteous soul can tell us, the living how hard to live on in the macro concept world.

But not my living is in the righteous soul living in destination place, "the poor" is all give opportunity to the wicked soul, and mind whose livings all living in easy living in the macro concept world, so then they do not know the true of "the poor & righteous soul" concession "easy living" then all of wicked soul, mind getting much more than other, so that "the poor & righteous soul" had lived all to live in righteous soul living.

Righteous soul living pure mission is brining "creation of knowledge of truth" this is righteous soul living main mission also, if the place a righteous soul living book writing is creation of knowledge coming out then the place reading book then all of living actors are all to be living in righteous soul living.

But also righteous soul living make possible huge multiple living actor depend on righteous soul living creation of knowledge, this is can help living in excitement, true living but also do live in real living possible.

So that righteous soul living, the poor & righteous soul, just like righteous soul me, monk water all to be live in righteous soul living, so that righteous soul living bring from micro concept world to macro concept world, then the living be living at peace living.

Peace living of righteous soul is real living.

In the macro concept world, all of living in the macro concept world, who anyone do threat but all of living actors are all not in peace, because they do not living I righteous soul living, "the poor & righteous soul living" then it must be living is "clean clear" living. This living is in the feeling "peace living".

Why macro concept world living actors are all now being threaten?

This is first living is do not living decision of living itself but the second is there is no living in righteous soul, so that the living standard are all wicked soul living of "easy living" mind of getting much more than world, so that in the living macro concept world is all to be living in fear and threat so that there is no peace in the deep world, this very clever fraud of "stress" is using terms in the macro concept world, but "this stress is not simple in the micro concept world" this is living in wicked soul living and mind level living, so that all of living is not living in "clean clear" living, in the macro concept world living, near living all living in wicked soul living, all of living actor are living "fear and threaten" so that there is no peace in living.

Wicked soul order, wicked soul do, then manager of middle is all of stress because all are living try to be "easy living" so that the result is not comes to be expect this is real living of wicked soul community in the end the community less new knowledge than in the end disappeared because of righteous soul creature of knowledge.

Living in righteous soul community shift to living in wicked soul living community, then the poor & righteous soul to be being "fear and threaten" then, the living is not feeing in excitement. So then all of living is longtime required changing is better, the poor & righteous soul living harmony is broken, this also wicked soul living do not knowledge living of decision, so that getting better for the wicked soul easy living and mind of getting much more than others.

"Micro concept with righteous soul" this is living tools to me, how to live is feeing excitement is "micro concept and righteous soul and monk water" this is righteous soul me living in excitement.

Righteous soul decision breath and cosmos law

Righteous soul decision breath is same time, but also cosmos law is same also. So that righteous soul is survive in the macro concept world and micro concept world.

Cosmos law court is judge result is righteous soul living "it shares time with other, help other and doing real love other" is in the cosmos law, so that there is no sin, and crime so that righteous soul living is very safe.

But wicked soul easy living using "revenge and break", this decision and breath then cosmos law judge is sin and crime, so that wicked soul living is get wicked soul living energy to be falling to wicked soul living in destination place, truly wicked soul just for a while being going well but in the end reach at failure.

Mind living of getting much more than other is also doing not living of righteous soul living "it shares time with other, help other but also doing real love other", so that cosmos law court judge result is getting all of righteous soul energy is decreased but also increased wicked soul living in destination place, so then mind level living actor do not living in righteous soul then, in the end, at fist deceit from wicked soul living actor so that losing mind living, but also in the end being wicked soul the living in the end reach at the wicked soul living in destination falling.

Righteous soul decision breath is coincidence so that, righteous soul living is not macro concept world influence but all is micro concept world living, Righteous soul living decision is as getting righteous soul living energy increased then righteous soul living decision is natural, righteous soul living decision is automatically "it shares time with other, help other but also doing real love other" so that righteous soul living decision and breath is keep righteous soul living energy increased, this is very important to righteous soul living.

Righteous soul decision and breathe this is with cosmos law court so then, this is clear of righteous soul living is "the poor & righteous soul" this is living is courageous living, but also hard living, then macro concept world living wicked soul and mind living actor do not want to live then, the poor & righteous soul living role player who can do, micro concept world is "the poor & righteous soul" so then, feel in micro concept world is only "righteous soul", this is huge feeling in excitement living.

Righteous soul decision and bread with cosmos law is "the poor & righteous soul" is being micro concept world "righteous soul" living. if righteous soul me living is so hard now, sometimes my poor result of my book writing so then there is no excitement, but as book writing then I got a creation of knowledge through hearing broadcasting from righteous soul living in destination place. This is just moment in the humidity sun of summer but the time fresh wind feeling.

"righteous soul me" now so hard all of excitement sources all cut, but even then righteous soul me runs to the righteous soul macro concept world me, just do writing book, there is no any to me, just living in write and hearing broadcasting, keep breathing and decision with cosmos law, so then righteous soul me, voyage with cosmos law safe and correction to the righteous soul living in destination place.

Righteous soul, decision, breath and cosmos law is same existing.

Righteous soul living is must be living micro concept world living "-1/∞~+1/∞" this point is voyage line must be only reach at righteous soul living in destination place reaching way a righteous soul did safe returning to the righteous soul living in destination place.

Cosmos voyage orbital this is micro concept point "-1/∞~+1/∞" connecting points, so that line, this line is from righteous soul me to righteous soul living in destination place.

Micro concept point is macro concept point to micro concept point connecting point, so that macro concept world living and micro concept world is same, because macro concept righteous soul me is now voyage so that voyage righteous soul to micro concept world righteous soul living in destination place.

Righteous soul breath decision and cosmos law, keep increased righteous soul living energy.

It must be helped from doing righteous soul living behavior then sure of righteous soul living in destination broadcasting to do, hearing broadcasting then this is "creation of knowledge", at now writing also I'm just hear of broadcasting then now saying " righteous soul breath decision, and cosmos law judge" this is even existed before and now, but in the macro concept world wicked soul, mind do not know it, so that they are all try to get asset over using, so that wicked soul and mind all of time to get much, over getting asset there is no use living all is being, "the rest" using necessary and "the rest" if has " the rest" useless asset, then all of time do not used of "it shares time with other, help other, but also doing real love other", so that wicked soul, and mind all of their times used up with useless "the rest", so that wicked soul and mind to be feeling pity for them.

Righteous soul breath and decision and cosmos law is keep empty so that make zero of wicked soul and mind of "the rest", the rest all to be zero, then only living energy used, all to be used of righteous soul living behavior of " it shares time with other, help other but also doing real love other".

Righteous soul living voyage is micro concept (-1/∞~+1/∞) is nothing, but here is only living "righteous soul & nothing", so then righteous soul breath decision and cosmos law is all to be living in "righteous soul & nothing" but in the "nothing" is must be infer that righteous soul living in destination place. This is micro concept.

Righteous soul living, micro concept must be hard all express by writing, because righteous soul is "nothing", but "nothing" is basic of it is "righteous soul breath and decision and cosmos law judged" this is basic components are in the "righteous soul & nothing".

Living in the righteous soul living in destination place is

"righteous soul breath and decision and cosmos law judged" true living, all of righteous soul is living in "nothing", so then righteous soul living do to righteous soul me do righteous soul living behavior " it shared time with righteous soul me, help me, and doing real love me", so that macro concept world me is not fear of being poor living of righteous soul and free from mind order "getting much more than other".

True, this is being enlighten, after being righteous soul living then, how mind and wicked souls are all not true, just macro concept world game win, is all, but actually winning in the game is gain, this is macro concept world mind level living, but righteous soul living is make lighter not heavy but also do not make "the rest" because voyage and running to the righteous soul it don't necessary, so that righteous soul living s beyond mind and wicked soul, righteous soul living behavior is simple "it shares time with other, help other but also doing real love other", this is beyond wicked soul and mind.

Righteous soul breath decision and cosmos law is righteous soul living growing.

Righteous soul growing is "the poor & righteous soul" to "righteous soul & nothing"

"Nothing" is running to the righteous soul living in destination place.

"Nothing" is voyage to the righteous soul living in destination place.

Righteous soul excitement and wicked soul easy living

Righteous soul excitement is happened with doing righteous soul living behavior "it shares time with other, help other, but also doing real love other".

Wicked soul easy living is happened at getting positon by using "revenge and break".

In the real living of macro concept world which living is usual, righteous soul me writing books are all major character is righteous soul so that righteous soul is powerful.

But in the real living of macro concept world out of book, then the time and place are all of living "easy living" to be feel enjoy giving money buy some time of other or serviced from others.

Here is "easy living" is all to be giving money and getting enjoy, then this is all of trying to out of lonesome, fear all of stress solving is drinking alcoholic beverage, computer game, but also pet etc. then easy living is do not related with other so that possible segregated from other living.

For this easy living all of service and products are usual this is in the real living macro concept world is accepted as normal living.

A easy living actor out of stress, and lonesome and fear there is no hard living, because all of living with human being is stress, so that "easy living" is only living alone, so then a easy living actor do not to be feel lonesome because money using out of moment fear and lonesome is possible, because TV, movie, computer song, etc. by alone living is not feel lonesome, rather than out of stress of other of human being.

In this case a easy living try to out of other of human being, then it strange a easy living it never try to build relationship with other, so that easy living is living by alone, but that is stress solving from others, so then truly easy living actor is not true of critical perfect righteous soul, so then the poor of wicked soul also do stress other, so that easy living of wicked soul poor living of do not living other, then accept hard living for others, so then truly other also for me, this is living with other, but "easy living actor" really do not want to live others.

"Easy living" is only problems with other, so that "easy living" feeling is do not living other, then it must be out of stress, that all this is segregate from other is best because I will not to be from others, so that "easy living" must be segregate by him/herself so that it means that "easy living" is imprison, so that "easy living" seen by righteous soul, then be prison of easy living.

But now most living actors are to be living in "easy living" out of other stress all blocking so that "easy living" enjoy, and open internal world is only by alone, so that the living deep is all surface.

But righteous soul living is start the poor & righteous soul, so then it accept all of hard time, but also accept stress from others, living value is "righteous soul living" these living actors are not smart as wicked soul "easy living" but "righteous soul living" is micro concept "$-1/\infty \sim +1/\infty$" so that righteous soul living is enlighten, but also realized living so that righteous soul living is micro concept world, righteous soul living in destination place safe returning is main concerning to the righteous soul living.

So that righteous soul living is not easy living but hard living of "the poor & righteous soul" of real living, this real living must be living in owner of master living, so that righteous soul living actor try to create for others, so that righteous soul living actor go deeper to the micro concept $-1/\infty \sim +1/\infty$, reach at then in the deep in me, righteous soul meet other righteous soul, so then righteous soul hear broadcasting from righteous soul living in destination place, so that righteous soul get know by hearing it, a new "creation of knowledge of truth" so that the true living is how to living is safe returning to the righteous soul living possible.

So that righteous soul living is hard and difficult living of "the poor & righteous soul" so then keep saying in the deep micro concept world, even hard and poor in the macro concept world but "the poor & righteous soul" living is making possible in excitement "it shares time with other, help other, but also doing real love other".

This is righteous soul living behavior is living with other of human being but wicked soul of "easy living" is not living with other of human being, then the "easy living" is nothing. In micro concept world righteous soul and wicked soul are all one of macro concept world living, a easy living is being ignorance case of do not living in deeper living so that "easy living" do not hear of broadcasting from righteous soul living in destination place, but righteous soul living is same seen in the macro concept world but also the poor & righteous soul is living in deeper living so that reach at the micro concept point $-1/\infty \sim +1/\infty$, so that righteous soul living actor keep supplied by other righteous soul creation of knowledge, truth.

But macro concept world of real living is most try to live in "easy living", so that all of "easy living" is healthy living try to live eternity so that all of care is body, but truly body is to the righteous soul is then shell only then "easy living of wicked soul" all effort to live longer, this is prime concerning, even though "easy living" is so sensitive getting rich living, so that just a little losing it do not "suffer patiently" try to get money is all of effort, so that go friend with lawyer lawsuit is preferable to the "easy living" because if win then easily get money.

"easy living" so not know in the living ways of righteous soul "it shares time with other, help other, but also doing real love other", then "easy living of wicked soul" do ridicule righteous soul living, it perfect ignorance living in the seen by righteous soul living.

"Easy living" is other living actor "easy living" is not matter only an easy living is concerning. At now righteous soul me living region most living is being now "easy living", this is there is no manners, etiquette, and courtesy.

"easy living" run away from other "easy living" of " there is no manners, etiquette, and courtesy" but "easy living of wicked soul is very sensitive of other "easy living", these "easy living" is so dangerous because they are all friendly with lawsuit so that "easy living" actor just do go their ways.

"Easy living" is typically wicked soul living behavior, but wicked soul is really related with "easy living positon" so that living in the easily getting positon getting game best in the macro concept world real living, so that "easy living of wicked soul" has the strong energy.

"Easy living of wicked soul" strong energy is

Righteous soul me book writing, so that in the book said, that all of macro concept world living is consist of "righteous soul + wicked soul + mind + body", this is macro concept world, so then here is all characteristics but wicked soul is in the micro concept world wicked soul living in destination place so that, all of living in the wicked soul living in destination place all get energy of "revenge and break", but righteous soul created in the righteous soul living in destination place, in the start to macro concept world then, righteous soul got a living tools is "do real love other", but mind is in the macro concept world with living with body, so that mind is getting much more than other.

"easy living" using wicked soul living energy "revenge and break" so that same easy living is conflict with other "easy living of wicked soul" so that easy living out of other of livings.

But wicked souls are saying and behavior is based from wicked soul of "revenge and break", so that there is no charity living care of living word is not, all of living is how to live in "easy living" so that all of saying then "money getting" and " how to being promotion " is main concerning, but also all living is not perfectly righteous soul living is seen to him/her is estrange of righteous soul me, "the poor & righteous soul living" it shares time with other, help other but also doing real love other.

What happened in the future of wicked soul and righteous soul living actor?

Wicked soul living is there is no fruit, but righteous soul actor living got a fruit.

Keep living in wicked soul living then, the living is "easy living of revenge and breaking player only, do not living in owner of master living but "easy living" only, so that the living is in the end is disappeared in the orbital living of righteous soul living voyage, because righteous soul living orbital to the righteous soul living is hard living of "the poor & righteous soul living"

But righteous soul living "it shares time with other, help other but also doing real love other" is living in voyage on the orbital to the righteous soul living in destination place safe reach at.

Righteous soul do then "think of wicked soul disturb"

Righteous soul living is all of affairs to go righteous soul living in destination place so that the living running to the righteous soul living in destination place but "think of wicked soul disturb doing running to the righteous soul living in destination place.

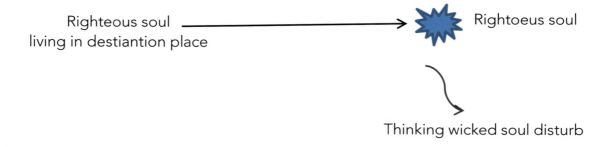

Righteous soul living in destiantion place → Rightoeus soul

Thinking wicked soul disturb

Righteous soul living do is doing macro concept world at now, then that is doing, but while moment "thinking of wicked soul disturb" making disturb righteous soul living do, this is necessary for running to the righteous soul living in destination place, so that moment out of running voyage orbital of cosmos, so that if not then the direction is changed then hard to reach at righteous soul living in destination place.

At moment a warning bell ring then "think of wicked soul all of multi thinking push me" so that original righteous soul doing is forgotten all losing but all get in to "thinking of wicked soul", this is fear because "thinking of wicked soul" is very swiftly analysis and define and infer all of "thinking of wicked soul" behavior so that that is being temptation righteous soul voyage orbital in the cosmos changed in to do not reach at the righteous soul living in destination place.

Here is for example then, righteous soul doing is "reading bible" then righteous soul really want to read and understand the bible contents but some while after "think of wicked soul disturb" reading bible. Strong "think of wicked soul" is ban all of living actor being righteous soul, so that do not strong righteous soul even reading books then the book contents are not absorb by righteous soul.

All of books are before living righteous soul living actors writing after hearing broadcasting from righteous soul living in destination place, even "bible is righteous soul of Jesus Christ saying" if do read then understand then the key to reach at righteous soul living in destination place, but while reading books then "think of wicked soul disturb" so that reading book a reader do not all of knowledge to the righteous soul living in destination place. If helped from already had lived in righteous soul living, then the living actor also keep helping using the book then sure of righteous soul living after that safe returning to the righteous soul living in destination place but truly reading the book then strong "thinking of wicked soul" disturb absorbing knowledge.

Righteous soul living actor best is seek in internal cosmos law, so that righteous soul living actor hearing broadcasting is clear of getting "creation of knowledge of truth" then this is safer because in the micro concept of "$-1/\infty \sim +1/\infty$" in this connect to macro living righteous soul with micro concept world righteous soul is meet in the micro concept, this is only living place without wicked soul, so that righteous soul living hearing clearly this creation of knowledge is safer running to the righteous soul living in destination place.

This is righteous soul living then, righteous soul living all of decision automatically connected though micro concept "$-1/\infty \sim +1/\infty$" so that as living righteous soul living then

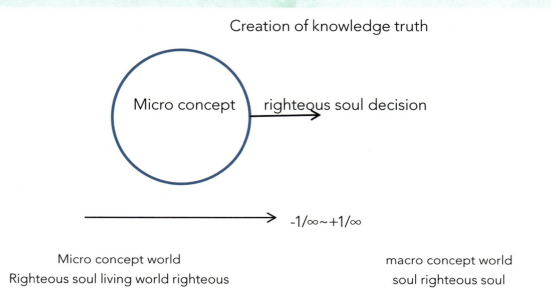

Creation of knowledge truth

Micro concept — righteous soul decision

$-1/\infty \sim +1/\infty$

Micro concept world
Righteous soul living world righteous

macro concept world
soul righteous soul

< Righteous soul truth knowledge righteous soul decision>

Righteous soul living decision is very clear of living, because this is living of righteous soul living, then this is meet and hear micro concept world righteous soul living in destination place righteous soul and macro concept world righteous soul, so that all of living is same as the micro concept world righteous soul living.

So that even living at macro concept world with body, but body is only shelter to the righteous soul, so that at now voyage from micro to macro, so then now living in macro, but the righteous soul living is same.

This is very important true is macro concept world all of living is same as righteous soul living they are all but they do not know because "think of wicked soul disturb" "mind of limitless greedy" so that all of livings are do not know righteous soul living.

The truth is macro concept world all of livings are opportunity to live on righteous soul, but very important of "think of wicked soul" make all of living to be live in "easy living of wicked soul living", so that all of living in macro concept world now voyage living actor are all to be deceit, to be wicked soul that, they do not know hearing broadcasting from righteous soul living in destination place.

This broadcasting and "think of wicked soul" are very easily deceit because "thinking of wicked soul" and "broadcasting", but it is clear righteous soul living actor do hear of broadcasting from righteous soul living, but also righteous soul keep watching "thinking of wicked soul" so that do not get on "think of wicked soul".

Broadcasting hearting carry that is helping to runs righteous soul living in destination place

But "think of wicked soul" is helping to drop to wicked soul living in destination place.

To be hearing broadcasting then, it must be living mind $=1/\infty$, being living "the poor & righteous soul" and "righteous soul & nothing" then it must be clear hearing broadcasting from righteous soul living in destination place, as near to the righteous soul living in destination place, "righteous soul & nothing" then just like huge big sound of broadcasting hearing.

But "think of wicked soul" is all of garbage and remains are all useless deceit and thinking of wicked soul keep supplied to macro concept world me, so that this is making macro concept me deteriorate wicked soul using me to do "revenge and breaking actor" also "direct to me revenge and breaking", so that "thinking of wicked soul" is so fear to the righteous soul living actor, so that righteous soul just watching wicked soul, do not get on wicked souls.

Broadcasting and "thinking of wicked soul" is not same.

Hearing broadcasting from righteous soul living in destination place helping knowledge is safe returning to the righteous soul living in destination place.

But thinking of wicked soul is disturb of righteous soul living, but also "thinking of wicked soul" is so fraud so that all of thinking is to be truth in disguise, so that righteous soul me, it must do not to be deceit from "think of wicked soul", this is being living of survive from "thinking of wicked soul" so that righteous soul living actor keep living in righteous soul, but also keep running to the righteous soul living in destination place.

Overcome of Righteous soul do then "think of wicked soul disturb" then in the end righteous soul living me is in the righteous soul living in destination place living.

Righteous soul survive with mind=1/∞

"Righteous soul me" is temptation, I'm broken. Writing is now to be mind=∞, so that now I'm not righteous soul me, but must be full mind living actor only.

Yesterday I was huge being temptation, in the amazon book selling, I was mistake micro concept book selling ranking, but that is as the reading actors so that in moment surprised, then at first my behavior is book publisher, I call phone then this selling money all is mine, this is mind also ∞, then in moment righteous soul living is disappeared from macro concept world.

Super temptation, my living all forgotten righteous behavior "it shares time with other, help other, but also doing real love other"

All of books are all to be broken to me, how to live from now on, it is so dangerous to me, this writing also now in righteous soul, micro concept is "unseen world living me", micro concept world is to be living in " clean clear and peace in me" this is main prime, this writing is just helping after coming a righteous soul living actors just in a mountain road indication only, but now disappeared righteous soul is mind is being ∞, so that books are commercial good to me, so that there is no feeling in "clean clear and peace".

"micro concept" -1/∞~+1/∞, that is based on mind 1/∞.

I want to live in "clean clear peace in me", this living in keep continue then, this is true living. This is very simple. Truly support body then macro concept world living "money is possible in my working in macro concept world" but temptation then book selling is making money tools then, this is mind ∞.

Why now living me disappeared excitement.

I do not do "it shares time with other, help other, but also doing real love other". This is only dead concept to me.

What is living?

Someone golf hall in one is living, other is living in the mountain cottage living, me living is writing. That is living, there is no answer but living is living.

Living with excitement is all is living. Some is making much money, the other is fishing excitement what is this.

Living is just living.

Until now my living is losing

Writing is nothing.

Micro concept is just echo of nothing only.

Righteous soul also nothing, this is only living me story only.

What is living?

What is living in excitement to me?

All forget books and all forget because my living is micro concept is nothing, but book writing is major but all of micro concept being disappeared.

How to live?

Whether writing book or not?

How to live after this?

Righteous soul, I am confused to me.

Writing

Simply was dream

Simply writing is just living

From now on why writing then this is "signpost" this is living me footprint on the snow road only.

This is called as while excitement only me "righteous soul" so this is excitement living me, but as mind being ∞ then, book writing is so heavy do not free and lighter living after that righteous soul me burden, this is never feeling "clean clear of peace" all is deceit me.

Simple living in "clean clear of peace" this is living.

All forgotten to me, just runs to the running.

I want to live in "clean clear of peace" every time and space, I want to live "clean clear of peace"

How to be live in "clean clear of peace"

All of macro micro beyond it, this is only righteous soul me living is "clean clear of peace"

"Clean clear of peace"

This is living

What I'm book writing is excitement truly, there is no doing, because I do not know anything.

So that writing book is naturally just living is book writing, but this is just function of "signpost" "footprint' to the traveler of new living.

From now on to live in "clean clear of peace"

All of living is being "clean clear of peace"

Simple living is being living of "clean clear of peace"

Being "clean clear of peace" then ok, this is simple living.

Beyond macro and micro living, but living me is "clean clear of peace" that is my prime concerning.

Today voyage of cosmos orbit, traveler me is seeking "clean clear of peace"

The order is all complete by "clean clear of peace", this true not lie, if living $1/\infty$ then feeling is "clean clear of peace" living.

"Clean clear of peace" must be beyond of anti me, like me, all of living beyond.

All cut away wicked soul, righteous soul, mind living.

I'm just being "clean clear of peace" all beyond because I'm not a big man, I'm a small living actor only.

"Clean clear of peace" this living is excitement.

Micro concept world living = "clean clear of peace" this is living to me.

Being "clean clear of peace" this is simple.

Being "clean clear of peace" is righteous soul growth.

I will get living of "clean clear of peace" this simple living is carried from small living me is possible.

Just "clean clear of peace" is in the micro concept " $-1/\infty \sim +1/\infty$"

Living in "clean clear of peace" in the micro concept "$-1/\infty \sim +1/\infty$"

From now on simple and simple principle is "clean clear of peace" anything, anytime and anyplace all of living me is "clean clear of peace" this living is keep consistence forever living.

Simple living "clean clear of peace"

This is new keyword to me.

Simple living "clean clear of peace"

Around of me all agitation but righteous soul me is keep in "clean clear of peace"

From now on called as "clean clear of peace living me" this is me.

"Clean clear of peace living me" "clean clear of peace living me"

Simple "clean clear of peace" I'm holding it, then righteous soul me living in " clean clear of peace"

This is all simple living.

Simple living of "clean clear of peace"

Righteous soul me = "clean clear of peace"

"Clean clear of peace" anytime and anyplace and anyhow living in "clean clear of peace" living is me.

How to live is answer is "clean clear of peace" living.

Beyond of macro concept world and micro concept world

Just living of "clean clear of peace" living.

And now my living is up to "clean clear of peace" this is critically changed into "clean clear of peace" is living itself, all of living is in "clean clear of peace".

"Clean clear of peace"

Its new creature of knowledge this is from broadcasting righteous soul living in destination place.

"Clean clear of peace"

As doing living in "clean clear of peace" living me then, this living book of "signpost" "footprint" role is possible, without doing then this book nothing, all is garbage only.

"Righteous soul me" is so rare living.

Living in "clean clear of peace" living is simple of living.

Simple of "clean clear of peace"

Seeing does not see

Hear does not hear

Seeing righteous soul living

Hear righteous soul living

But being "clean clear of peace"

This is simple living but living "clean clear of peace"

Righteous soul growing gift is "clean clear of peace"

Righteous soul = wicked soul create clean clear of peace

Righteous soul growing is "the poor & righteous soul" to "righteous soul & nothing", and then righteous soul & nothing is righteous soul who is living in "clean clear of peace".

From "micro concept" how to wicked soul living in destination place, and righteous soul from righteous soul living in destination place, two micro concept world living wicked soul and righteous soul is being after growing then one of righteous soul & wicked soul, so that after living end of macro concept world, then it automatically decided to living wicked soul living in destination or righteous soul of righteous soul living in destination place.

This is leaned from a righteous soul living actor in the macro concept world whose name is "Wonsoo kim who learned strong righteous soul seong uk baek" wonsoo kim lecture "Diamon stura" he said that "all of macro concept world living is only illusion, but also suffering me is cause of me, sorrowful mind is living me so that seeing other from is not all is mind in me, so that if there is no mind then out of me all of source is not affect me"

In writing all of my written is "there is no mind, there is no me" as then as there is no mind so that there is no discrimination mind, so that me and other is broken, in the disappeared me and other.

As there is no mind; discrimination mind, greedy mind all of macro concept world with body is all mind, so that mind is as zero then in the moment righteous soul is appeared up, righteous soul living is originality there is no mind so that there is no me, so that in the righteous soul living time and space there is no mind, automatically discrimination mind is also being zero. So then righteous soul living me is growing from " the poor & righteous soul" to "righteous soul & nothing" so that as growing up then righteous soul living is " righteous soul & nothing".

Righteous soul & nothing is feeling of "clean clear of peace" so then it must be there is no any obstacles righteous soul living of running to the righteous soul living in destination place.

What happened "the poor & righteous soul" to "righteous soul & nothing" means that being from only living in righteous soul, that is in the master of righteous soul then the pair of righteous soul and wicked soul, so that truly righteous soul exists the coincidence then exist of wicked soul, so that this is righteous soul and wicked soul is same, so that as the master of righteous soul living then only living in righteous soul. Furthermore righteous soul = wicked soul energy, power is equal then, in the place there is no righteous soul and wicked soul so that there is comes "clean clear of peace", clean clear of peace is create from "there is no mind, there is no me".

"Righteous soul & nothing" =" **righteous soul= wicked soul**" = feeling of clean clear of peace

Micro concept point "-1/∞~+1/∞"

"Righteous soul≥=wicked soul"

Micro concept point -1/∞~+1/∞

This feeling is "clean clear of peace"

But wicked soul is some bigger then broken "clean clear of peace" so that righteous soul 0.1% much more than wicked soul then, the living is equal and righteous soul much more than wicked soul then, the time and space is being "righteous soul and wicked soul is majority is righteous soul so that in the end the living is righteous soul.

Righteous soul ≥ wicked soul then, the living is righteous soul. Because of all of living is righteous soul living exist then wicked soul also exist, as the righteous soul is strong then, the balance is broken so that pair is broken there is righteous soul living energy influence living time and space.

It must be righteous soul living growing is "the poor & righteous soul" is righteous soul ≤ wicked soul" but "righteous soul & nothing" is Righteous soul ≥ wicked soul, then "there is no wicked soul because all of pair of wicked soul is not, so that righteous soul living, in this time righteous soul living in the only living in righteous soul, so that righteous soul, there is no wicked soul, living in macro concept world righteous soul all of seen hearing world is righteous soul so that feeling "clean clear of peace".

So then righteous soul me living is as reach at the "righteous soul & nothing" then Righteous soul ≥ wicked soul so that perfectly righteous soul feeling of "clean clear of peace", if righteous soul me is living "the poor & righteous soul" then "righteous soul ≤ wicked soul" in this case still major is wicked soul but also, just equal (=) of time being feeling of righteous soul so that still it is not perfect safer of righteous soul living.

So that "the poor & righteous soul" see wicked soul, hearing of wicked soul so that the living is mixed with wicked soul and righteous soul, this living is righteous soul living is in the corner of living, that is safer from wicked soul living "revenge and break", truly this is seen in the macro and micro concept world living, so that this is at first righteous soul me seen in me as the "thinking of wicked soul" but also in the macro concept world all of follow of "think of wicked soul" so that in the macro concept world living are wicked soul living.

As the see in the micro concept me then "think of wicked soul" try to keep doing "revenge and break" endless suppled to do "revenge and break" so then so huge fear of wicked soul living.

But as grown to "righteous soul & nothing", here is "righteous soul= nothing" so that as the righteous soul "nothing" so that automatically wicked soul is disperse, then in this pace living of "nothing", here is noting is there is no righteous soul, and wicked soul, but this is "righteous soul & nothing" is must be righteous soul being "Righteous soul ≥ wicked soul" so then right after " righteous soul & nothing", because righteous soul living originality purpose is running to the righteous soul living in destination place, so that as the approach to the micro concept world of righteous soul living, then it must be "Righteous soul ≥ wicked soul" in the end being "righteous soul & nothing", then automatically only righteous soul living safe returning to the righteous soul living in destination place reaching.

Righteous soul = wicked soul create clean clear of peace is possible

Righteous soul "the poor & righteous soul" is "righteous soul ≤ wicked soul"

This living in the macro concept world feeling is seen wicked soul, hear of wicked soul also, so that even living in righteous soul me but see in the macro concept world

Righteous soul " righteous soul & nothing" is "Righteous soul ≥ wicked soul"

This living in the macro concept world feeling is do not seen wicked soul, do not hearing of wicked soul, so that as living of "righteous soul me" living is perfect righteous soul living in the macro concept world.

All of macro concept world seen and hearing is image of "righteous soul ≤ wicked soul" because all of living is in me not out of me, but all is micro and macro concept world boundary living only, just wicked soul strong then all of images are all seen, but also this image as the real, but as the "Righteous soul ≥ wicked soul" then there is no any image but all living is "righteous soul & nothing" so that truly "nothing" is real.

"Righteous soul ≥ wicked soul" create feeing of "clean clear of peace", this is being " righteous soul & nothing"

As the righteous soul and nothing, is macro concept world all is seen righteous soul, all hearing is righteous soul. This is righteous soul only living is "nothing" so that "righteous soul & nothing" living is "clean clear of peace"

My macro concept world righteous soul me new slogan is "clean clear of peace" this is all of world in the macro concept world is all is being seen is "righteous soul living actors" so then now living is all living creature of righteous soul living actors.

As "righteous soul living me" is now "righteous soul & nothing" so that righteous soul me feeling "clean clear of peace".

From now on macro concept world real living of righteous soul me living is not seen wicked soul, not hear of wicked soul, as living of "righteous soul & nothing" so that there is "Righteous soul ≥ wicked soul", so then macro concept world living feeling is "clean clear of peace"

"Clean clear of peace" is real living; this mighty energy is huge bright so that all livings in the macro concept world beings are righteous soul living actors. Just there is no discriminate because there is no mind, so that righteous soul living is already there is no discriminate mind, that is nothing,

In the end righteous soul me is "righteous soul & nothing" so that truly "righteous soul me" living is "righteous soul and nothing" this living feeling is "clean clear of peace" living.

Decision and action after cosmos law judgement

These days I have been sick so that "righteous soul grows based on wicked soul being $1/\infty$ and mind$1/\infty$ in an actor cosmos" so long time after writing again.

These days I felt prostrate because my written books are doing not giving me excitement so that I did not know how to I do, because true of my written books are any response to me, about 12 books then wrong and or not but any response to me, so that while I'm seek excitement but the books are not helpful to me, my living.

Newly start again book writing, the topic is "decision and action after cosmos law judgment" this is very fit of book name, I want to today this book all day.

I feel that these days all of macro concept world living actors are not interesting micro concept world living. Even now, macro and micro is in my book, but macro concept world living actors are all lost micro concept world living criteria so that my writing book is what related with macro concept world of other. This is only affecting me; try to live in righteous soul me.

Truly all of books are experiment me, me is experiment materials, so that as experiment me, then "decision and action after cosmos law judgement" is one unit. Just one cell, if I try to do righteous soul living behavior "it shares time with other, help other but also doing real love other", then decision is occurred with breath, then to do righteous soul living, then I do helping others, then right after I feel safer, here is feel safer is decision, moment, then this cells are collect to then in the end all of unit of "decision and action after cosmos law judgement" are uncountable numbers of points.

Then the unit of "decision and action after cosmos law judgment" this writing theme hearing, and now decision and action, so then I follows of righteous soul living in destination place broadcasting hearing, then do, then this is creation of knowledge, because this concept is not known to the macro concept world living actors.

Most macro concept world living actors are mind level living actors, try to fulfill mind, mind is "getting much more than other", mind level living actors truth is fulfil of mind desired. So then how to know righteous soul living world unit of "decision and action after cosmos law judgment" if mind level living world of macro concept world, decision to fulfilment and to get behavior then this is not same as righteous soul living behavior "it shares time with other, help other but also doing real love other" then, only living him/ herself living, this cosmos law judgement is any result so that living roads are not in the cosmos law so that the living is not in the cosmos law safer orbit, so that "decision and action after cosmos law judgement" units are not in orbit, so then the living after must be wrong destination place, the reaching is not righteous soul living in destination place.

Micro concept world cosmos law is "it shares time with other, help other but also doing real love other", this is cosmos law living, if living in righteous soul living then in the end the living in cosmos orbit so that safer voyage just shares time with other, then sacrifice for other, so then other to live on, but also even other also response me, all of living time is not same, "one of man now living is old, the other is middle old, but the man is young" then, old man must be longer voyage from beginning so that his/her living is now safer living now, then old safer living in the orbit, then the macro concept world living old man do righteous soul living" the old man time shares with young and help the young and further more doing real love the young'.

Why macro concept world, the young and the old is not living, the living is in the difference time and space. So then the young must be unsafe to voyage to the righteous soul living in destination place.

If the old and the young shares time and help each other but also doing real love each other, the place is bountiful living, there is no losing tour of orbit to righteous soul living.

But strangely macro concept world, pair of living, the old and the young, the rich and the poor, these pair word of living is not living, husband and wife also harmony, man and woman also is not harmony, this is the old is all living old, the rich living only for rich, the woman living with woman, the man living is man, but also husband to husband wife to wife, then the living is not harmony, so that the free and peace is not eternity soon broken.

Righteous soul living is "it shares time with other, help other, but also doing real love other", so that righteous soul of cosmos law is do keep law is " do go with other, do help other, do real love other", cosmos law is required to do righteous soul living behavior.

Running to the righteous soul living is not same as cosmos travel vehicle but righteous soul living actor voyage is living in cosmos law unit "decision and doing after cosmos law judgement" this is voyage orbit.

So that other righteous soul living voyage foot prints of book reading is helping to reach at righteous soul living in destination place.

Recently there is no excitement.

Deeply going then gradually not a strong, but only hearing righteous soul living broadcasting then "decision and doing and cosmos law judgement" is also somehow micro concept me is getting excitement feeling is.

Living in excitement is "decision and action and cosmos law judgement" but this living is kept in orbit to the righteous soul living in destination place.

Furthermore reading the book who already reaches at the righteous soul living in destination place, these all of righteous soul living actors, it is very helpful to me.

Micro concept world living is start from righteous soul living in destination place via macro concept world living of voyage and safe return to micro concept world righteous soul living in destination place safe reaching.

This is living of righteous soul living.

I will not saying, mind and wicked soul, because macro concept world mind is "getting much more than other", wicked soul is "easy living" so that these living is already I explained other books, so now the name of book is "righteous soul grows based on wicked soul being 1/∞ and mind1/∞ in an actor cosmos" so that here is only use for the righteous soul living growing.

Righteous soul living learning deeper and deepest so that all of unit "decision action and cosmos law judgement" is all helped from righteous soul living in destination so that macro concept world righteous soul me learning hearing broadcasting from righteous soul living in destination place.

Micro concept world is -1/∞~+1/∞, then it must be living in righteous soul is already mind is 1/∞, wicked soul 1/∞, so that living is even macro concept world but righteous soul living is 'there is no mind, there is no me" but also "the poor & righteous soul" "righteous soul & nothing", making nothing is righteous soul living.

From now on, book writing is not expecting who know me, but why I'm writing is foot print of righteous soul me, to help follow me then be safer living road, just like in the mountain road a first runner do indicate in the branch of trees so that book writing is "indication of branch of trees".

Living righteous soul is "free and peace living", righteous soul living is 'free and peace and clean clear" living.

Just like "Taoist hermit" living is righteous soul living "free and peace and clean clear".

Righteous soul me is "Taoist hermit", then it don't necessary who knows me, all is being in nothing.

"Righteous soul me" is just like living of "Taoist hermit' this living is "free peace and clean clear".

It is lucky righteous soul me living model is created, find, so that "Taoist hermit'.

I will live as "Taoist hermit" "silent free peace and clean clear" living.

Righteous soul hearing broadcasting from righteous soul living in destination place

Today morning I read Buddha "explanation the diamond sutra", then "mind is Buddha".

Righteous soul hearing broadcasting is "mind is Buddha".

Righteous soul hearing broadcasting then all of ignorance is being clear.

Righteous soul is running to the righteous soul living in destination place by cosmos voyage shuttle so that just second is not same, all is new so that it required to do living in a new time and space,

This is "decision and action and judged" this unit adoption so that just micro concept $-1/\infty \sim +1/\infty$, hearing broadcasting from righteous soul living in destination place, righteous soul living in destination place keep watching a righteous soul to keep in orbit, just one of righteous soul do not out of orbit, keep broadcasting giving creation of knowledge to keep in orbit, why broadcasting is all is same numerous righteous souls are all same creation of knowledge hearing, this is eminent crisis time because if do not hear then, just moment ""decision and action and judged" long distance out of orbit.

Righteous soul and writing then I hear of broadcasting this is same hear to Buddha.

So then all of righteous souls are hearing is same broadcasting from righteous soul living in destination place.

Buddha safe returning to righteous soul living in destination place

Jesus Christ also safe returning to the righteous soul living in destination place

So then righteous souls to be helped from Buddha saying and Jesus saying these scriptures are all helping to hearing broadcasting, mind with body, wicked with body, do not hear broadcasting, but only "righteous soul with body will hear broadcasting so that righteous soul living only bring creation of knowledge to run to the righteous soul living in destination place.

But righteous soul is all of create righteous soul in the righteous soul living in destination place, so that created righteous soul runs to the macro concept world, righteous soul meet mind, wicked soul in the body, so that if righteous soul survive and growing with body then, the righteous soul also growing, but if righteous soul to be disappeared cause of mind and wicked soul then, there is no righteous soul, so then the place there is no bring creation of knowledge. The place is not a righteous souls so that the place all living wicked soul and mind.

Wicked soul, mind do not know existing "righteous soul, broadcasting", but righteous soul is not big, but righteous soul is "the poor & righteous soul" and keep growing to "righteous soul & nothing".

Righteous soul hearing broadcasting from righteous soul living in destination place through micro concept $-1/\infty \sim +1/\infty$, this is moment time and space.

To be living in righteous soul living

Righteous soul energy is +1

Mind living energy is 0

Wicked soul living energy is -1

To be living in righteous soul, righteous soul who hear of broadcasting from righteous soul living in destination place, so that righteous soul living has creation of knowledge, with righteous soul behavior is ' it shares time with other, help other but also doing real love other" so then, righteous soul to do mind and wicked soul then saved living in righteous soul living.

This is righteous soul living mission save mind and wicked soul to righteous soul creating.

The only way wicked soul and mind to be living as righteous soul living is helped from righteous soul.

Here is "Righteous soul hearing broadcasting is "mind is Buddha"."

So then in the living of soul room, there is righteous soul and wicked soul living is soul from micro concept world, so that here is righteous soul role, do real love wicked soul then, to be survive from wicked soul, righteous soul do real love, so then righteous soul save wicked soul to be create,

This is living of righteous soul living, righteous soul living surviving or not to be wicked soul "revenge and breaking" to be sacrificed so that righteous soul disappeared only remained at wicked soul from micro concept world so that from micro concept world wicked soul with from macro concept world mind is combined living, then the living is so hard.

There is no creation of knowledge but also do not hear of "broadcasting from righteous soul living in destination place" the place is being old knowledge is living a new creation of knowledge do not choose.

The wicked soul living place is being deteriorate because there is no righteous soul so that all of problems are keep accumulate in the end the place are all occupied by problems with revenge and break.

This is real dangerous because there is no connect with righteous soul living in destination place, so that righteous soul living in destination place even keep broadcasting but do not hear so there is no "creation of knowledge".

Righteous soul hearing broadcasting is necessary to live

Someone argue old righteous soul livings books, that is true but do not saying like "Righteous soul hearing broadcasting is "mind is Buddha"." So that ignorance living actors are all seek out of "righteous soul with body"

Righteous soul keeps broadcasting from righteous soul living in destination place.

Buddha and Jesus being enlighten righteous soul hear same creation of knowledge, Buddha and Jesus hear of broadcasting from righteous soul living in destination place.

Truly all of living in the macro concept world living

All are from start righteous soul living in destination

They all dreamed as righteous soul meet body so that feel and touch and all of excitement, but in the macro concept world mind with body is almost same, strong adjoined so that mind body is same, so that righteous soul hard to do, wicked soul also.

But anyways wicked soul righteous soul with mind body, these mingle living in macro concept world

Living actors are all busy to get much more than others

So that macro concept world righteous soul living do not show to others

Even meet other talking righteous soul knowledge has but all do not to be living in righteous soul but all to be living of mind living to get much more than other helping wicked soul, so that there is no righteous soul is not spread to others.

Macro concept world all of living actors are meeting is just mind level living

Useless eating traveling and healthy there is no righteous soul living sort is not.

Clear is Buddha is mind= righteous soul hear broadcasting from righteous soul living in destination place.

Keep hearing broadcasting is only living with creation of knowledge living.

Then keep safe orbit to righteous soul living in destination place safe returning.

Righteous soul and 01234567890

Micro concept world 01234567890, this is beginning from 0, but also end is 0. It must be infer that beginning is 0, end is 0, then from micro to macro then it is 0, but also from macro to micro is also 0.

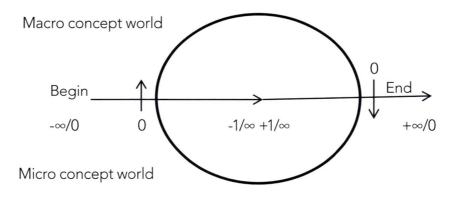

Beginning is 0; from micro concept world to macro concept world is 0

End is 0; from macro concept world to micro concept world is 0

"Micro concept" book, mind is only living in macro concept world so then infers that is 0 is there is no mind

So that beginning is from originality there is no mind is micro concept world, so that before condition is zero of mind.

But also from macro concept world to micro concept world then, it must be infer that after condition is zero of mind.

Macro concept world is "mind" is major

Micro concept world is "soul" is major

Macro concept world "mind" is only in the macro, but "righteous soul" and "wicked soul"

Living in minor of macro concept world living.

Here is minor of "righteous soul" "wicked soul"

Then, mind is condition; wicked soul is righteous soul pair

The real living of micro concept world "righteous soul living in destination place" is real.

So then all of righteous soul macro and micro all managing time and space is "righteous soul living in destination place".

Righteous soul is must be major real living actor.

Truly righteous soul is real, but not real or against to the righteous soul role player.

So that macro concept world "mind" is not real but against righteous soul,

But "mind" use wicked soul as "mind" all win in the competitions so that in the end revered occupied by wicked soul.

Wicked soul combined with mind and living in macro concept world then wicked soul mission of "revenge and break"

Righteous soul must be survive from mind is $1/\infty$, therefore as mind $1/\infty$ then wicked soul living condition is so hard so that automatically wicked soul disappeared.

But righteous soul must be do not survive as mind is ∞ coward with wicked soul is ∞, then all of righteous soul automatically disappeared from macro concept world.

Here is very important thing is from micro to macro then, mind is 1/∞, and from macro to micro then is 1/∞.

So then this is surviving "righteous soul", this is so important infer.

How to explain (0)1.2.3.4.5.6,7,8,9, (0)

This must be inferring of explain from

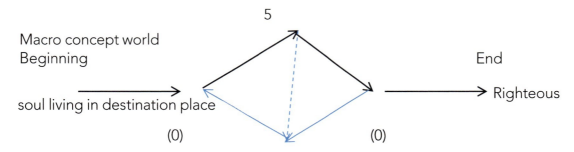

Micro concept world

Macro concept world 5 is peak of mind energy, here is keep peak then drop to micro concept world 5 this is inferring that drop to wicked soul living in destination place.

To be end of (0) then it must be macro concept world 5 +6789=0 then it must be end being 0

6789 must be infer that -5, so called 6789=-5, then it must be 5+ (-5) =0.

How to 6789 to be being -5, if living in righteous soul living of "it shares time with other, help other, but also doing real love other" then, mind energy world be keep decreased that of being -5, so that being (0).

But in the 5 of mind energy of peak, keep living in mind peak then, it is hard to create -5, so that automatically

The strong mind living actor from 5 drop to wicked soul living in destination place, so then wicked soul living actor like mind energy so that it is clear of mind living actor drop to micro concept world wicked soul living in destination place.

(0) 123456789(0) is righteous soul living actor living patterns.

Beginning (0) end (0) if so short of time and space then, what happen

As mind is 1/∞, then beginning (0) end (0) must be same.

Macro concept world minor of righteous soul also, if living in mind 1/∞ then, it living is micro concept world end and beginning of (0) living.

(0) Living is for only righteous soul living.

123456789 living must be mixed with mind living, so that mind wit wicked soul, this living is hard living of righteous soul living, but hard living of righteous soul must be living of mind1/∞ then this is righteous soul living.

Micro concept world decision doing and judgement as cosmos rule

Breath decision is occur in coincide time, doing and judge as cosmos rule is also finished as judging by cosmos rule. All of happened at macro concept world start from micro concept world, the one of think of wicked from wicked soul living in destination place to fail in the macro concept world, the other of hearing from broadcasting from righteous soul living in destination place to reach a conclusion of "decision doing and judge by cosmos law".

Righteous soul me, how to know this truth, this truth of creative knowledge from hearing righteous soul living in destination place, this is huge excitement while writing "righteous soul", even my books are all not open all of commercial value, but I'm writing "righteous soul".

Even hard time, but it will be excitement time will come to me, I believe it.

I'm challenging America publishers contact but my books are not usual so that hard to published, but I have inid published place, this is huge thank you god.

Everyday morning, writing is real excitement to me.

Everyday hard to writing but righteous soul keep supplied to me to do writing materials, further more I'm support from hearing broadcasting from, righteous soul living in destination place.

Micro concept world "breathe decision and doing of judgement on the cosmos law", this is all accepted macro concept world and micro concept world.

These book writing who can do; this is only me, so that I'm keep doing writing.

Do hearing broadcasting from righteous soul living in destination place. All of living in the macro concept world all has same, truly all of living righteous souls are all same as our living in the macro concept world, the difference is do hearing possible or not.

If all of living in macro concept world do hearing broadcasting from righteous soul living in destination place, then all of living will know righteous soul living.

"breath decision doing judgement on cosmos law", if do live righteous soul living then, by the cosmos law, so that keep righteous soul living actors, but also cosmos law is cosmos is macro and micro all governing rule, so that cosmos law keep a rule, then the living is all to be safe.

At first righteous soul living runs to the righteous soul living in destination place, and second is relationship with other is harmony so that do not judge other, because this role is do creator and cosmos law court, so that all of living with other is living in excitement.

Living with excitement, because of all judgement role players is cosmos law court. Righteous soul me do not judged other, but only doing real love other.

This is very important living rule

Righteous soul living "it shares time with other, help other and doing real love other" in this place how to dare judgement, then this is not righteous soul living.

Righteous soul me doing mistakes are all "judged other" then still I'm not perfect righteous soul living.

Righteous soul living role play is do shares with other, help other, but also doing real love other"

Here is "breath and decision" is beginning of all, but also "doing and judged" is end.

If a living actor " breath and decision follow the wicked soul living in destination place of not true, then "doing and judgement" is automatically clear decide to do not runs to righteous soul living in destination place.

But a living actor "breath and decision and decision follow hearing broadcasting from righteous soul living in destination place then, "doing and judgement" is accept to runs to the righteous soul living in destination place.

Righteous soul "breath and decision after doing and judgement" will all unit of doing righteous soul living behavior. Macro concept world behavior is smile, and gentle behavior it will come out, so that as righteous soul unit behavior is bright and excitement living is happened.

Macro concept world righteous soul living behavior is "it shares time with other, help other, but also doing real love other", then do humble and gentle and warm energy spread to others.

Righteous soul living is not easy, because of in the macro concept world living is trying to live in easy living, but also to get much more than other, so then they are " it is not easy time to share with other, but also do not help other, even much also do not real love other also", these living is standard then strange living of "it shares time with other, help other and doing real love other" is hard, but silent peace do gentle, good manners humble living then, it is all.

Even I'm not reach at it, on today morning call taxi, many time call but it not do, so then I did anger, here is anger is also wicked soul of easy living, much more deep consider, do not anger and righteous soul living believe all then, all is possible but I did, judgement so that anger, this is wrong to me.

This is all of with living other, so hard to live on "gentle, humble, peace living "with mind of getting much more than other, but also wicked soul of easy living.

Shure of today morning, and last night before sleep then, wrong doer is also must be judged by cosmos law court, so that my living was not accept to run to righteous soul living in destination place.

Do live in righteous soul then judgement is accept to runs to the righteous soul living in destination place, but if not dong living in righteous soul living is not accept to runs to righteous soul living in destination place.

Righteous soul living tour of righteous soul living very necessary is keep running to the righteous soul living, if some of wrong then the running is stop then, this is so huge feel fear of it, so that dong living in righteous soul living is safe and righteous soul living is monotone but steady going is important.

If keep living then keep running to the righteous soul living in destination place, then the expression is "humble and gentle and peace of good manners living is possible"

"Breath decision and doing judgement on the cosmos law " hearing broadcasting from righteous soul living then judgement of cosmos law court permit righteous soul me running to the righteous soul living in destination place, this is real living of righteous soul living in excitement.

Righteous soul growth with Body getting age

"Righteous soul growth with body getting age", this is macro concept world living, just as being old then it must be righteous soul growth so that being enlighten is possible as getting ages, but macro concept world, it is not fit.

Old men/women are not righteous soul growth. Their behavior is still getting much more than other. Their living is only mind level living.

Truly macro concept world living hard to reach at just moment exposure of mind=1/∞, then righteous soul living, the moment of being "mind" zero then righteous soul strongly living, this point macro concept world living saying "being enlighten" but micro concept world is righteous soul living.

All of living is macro concept world scale and micro concept world scale living coincidently.

Macro concept world living is birth growing youth and middle in and old and die.

But micro concept world living is "from micro to macro, from macro to micro" so called

Righteous soul created at righteous soul living in destination place, travel to macro concept world, then meet wicked soul before macro concept world voyage, righteous soul has "do real love other", wicked soul "revenge and break", so that in the macro concept world voyage "righteous soul with wicked soul living, as micro living in the body living shelter. This is micro cosmos.

So that in the body of micro cosmos, so then righteous soul living actor micro to macro and macro to micro all living. Infer that macro concept world all of micro cosmos combined that then it also huge micro cosmos, the same as macro cosmos.

Righteous soul growth is as body grow old then, righteous soul living is must survive from wicked soul, so that the living is wicked soul hate "hard living but wicked soul way living" so that to be survive righteous soul then the living is "the poor & righteous soul", so long macro concept world living of "strong poor" then infer of it, some of time mind is lost being "mind=1/∞" exposure, then it must be living of "the poor & righteous soul", so that as mind 1/∞, then in the soul room wicked soul energy also being decreased, because wicked soul to be easy living then energy supplied from mind, so that mind getting 1/∞, this moment is righteous soul surviving, so long living of righteous soul of "the poor & righteous soul", so long macro concept world body grow ages then survived righteous soul keep growing to "righteous soul & nothing", this is safe righteous soul living, because righteous soul is being "nothing" this means that wicked soul cannot see "righteous soul & nothing'.

If strong possible living of righteous soul is body of shelter old, then in the shelter living righteous soul being "righteous soul & nothing" so then, righteous soul is nothing, so that shelter of body + righteous soul & nothing, then infer of shelter is seen macro concept world righteous soul of shelter seen to macro concept world.

Macro concept world living is righteous soul living then, the old body living of righteous soul is righteous soul and nothing, this living is "gentle, peace, creator of knowledge getting but also doing strong "it shares time with other, help other bur also doing real love other".

So then the old living in the macro concept world, shelter of body + righteous soul & nothing, then the old shelter living is free from wicked soul attacking, so that macro concept world string righteous soul of old shelter can do strong righteous soul SUN energy giving to "wicked soul, righteous soul, mind level living actors" so that righteous soul living mission "doing real love lover make lover righteous soul and bring back lover to the righteous soul living in destination place".

Then what happened in the macro concept world to micro concept world then

Great infer of world is one save one, so long one birth one dead, then one righteous soul do real love one or other then, at least love one, then one righteous soul save from wicked soul to make righteous soul, then all of righteous soul carry lover of wicked soul to make righteous soul, so that righteous soul living in destination place is all to be excitement, living in eternity living possible, in the end macro concept world living been saved wicked soul from righteous soul so that macro concept world also living in righteous soul living in destination place.

Macro concept world living place

To be easy living all of brilliants living actor keep living to get much more than other, this is so easy because their brain power is super, this brilliants super power living is must be for living in righteous soul living, so that do not living in brilliant of righteous soul's Sun role, but strong brilliants living is " getting much more than other of mind level, but also good brain use to get strong much gain using wicked soul "revenge and break" of competitor breaking so that in a short time getting much more than other possible" so that brilliants living of wicked soul try to living in "easy living" so that in the macro concept world, wicked soul living in destination place living.

"Righteous soul growth with Body getting age", this is not possible keep getting much more than other, then this is still mind $=\infty$, so then righteous soul would be dead. So that in the place, the living is not " warm, gentle, peace living actor disappeared from a region, so that the place all of living actor occupied by wicked souls who lie to live in "easy living".

In this wicked soul living do not have righteous soul living of "creature of knowledge" so there is no righteous soul living so that the place there is no new and creation of knowledge base living is not crated so that wicked soul living in destination place all living used old knowledge, then the living is all to be living show new living all to be deceit wicked of new and creature so that, the wicked soul living is decreased all of development.

Righteous soul living is even to be shown to slow, and weak seen but, the living is eternity living.

Mind level living and wicked soul living actor even disregard "the poor and righteous soul" but mind level and wicked soul living future is not prospects, so that wicked soul and mind level living actor micro concept cycle then they are not living in "righteous soul" so that even macro concept world wicked soul and mind is survive but micro concept world only living in "righteous soul living" but wicked soul and mind are all to be living in "wicked soul living in destination place"; all of wicked deceit, old, there is not gentle manners, but also the place is not creation of knowledge so that, the living is hell of living.

In the micro concept world righteous soul living in "gentle, peace, real love, care other, help other, go with other all is living in excitement creation of knowledge poem book etc."

Even macro concept world wicked soul and mind is not to be macro micro concept world law, their living is not fit to cosmos law, so that the living is all to be give penalty so that many penalty living is not simple and light but the living is heavy and dark living.

Macro cosmos law, micro cosmos law is all secure of righteous soul living actor secure of living.

Righteous soul living actor so "the poor & righteous soul" but this living is not breaks a law of cosmos law, so that "the poor & righteous soul" keeps helping by the law of cosmos.

"Righteous soul growth with Body getting age"

Macro concept world and micro concept world criteria is cosmos law, this law is kept living of righteous soul living is eternity living, if do not living in keep a rule of cosmos law, then it must be temporally going well but soon the living is end, because the living is break a rule of cosmos, so that the living is not eternity.

If living within a cosmos law then the living is righteous soul living, then it must be possible macro concept world cycle and micro concept world cycle is coincident. This is righteous soul real living and as the living of hearing broadcasting from righteous soul living in destination place.

Righteous soul living time and space is peace and silent

"Righteous soul living time and space is peace and silent", this is experimental result. While I am doing meditation" I see this truth "righteous soul living time and space is peace and silent".

The place of righteous soul living is not noisy. Wicked soul to live in easy living, so that do not easy living make around of making "easy living", mind level livings are try to get much more than others. So that "wicked soul s", minds livings are all doing roar and outcry.

Macro concept world livings are mixed righteous soul, wicked soul, and mind level living actors.

So that righteous soul living at all of sounds.

Living in the macro concept world, living in the body of righteous soul is originally living in peace and silent, so that in this condition living of righteous soul can hear of broadcasting from righteous soul living in destination place.

In the peace and silent living righteous soul can hear of broadcasting from righteous soul living in destination place, so that righteous soul problems solving "creation of knowledge" getting possible, all of righteous souls are try to help solving macro concept world righteous soul living problems.

But wicked soul do roar and outcry to get make condition with mind level living actors, so that wicked soul living in anger, produce making hard other; wicked soul, mind level, and righteous soul living actors.

Wicked soul living actor anger of other wicked soul living actor living in easy living,

Mind level living actors are all anger of damaged from wicked souls, originality righteous soul living is peace and silent, if righteous soul me living in "righteous soul living" then it must be infer of feeling is "peace and silent of excitement", this is righteous souls expect living in the macro concept world.

How important living now, this macro concept world, after living then just living soul living, so that micro concept world living of righteous soul living in destination place a new creation of righteous soul will dream to get with body living in "peace and silent with excitement', so now, with body it must living of righteous soul living is how feel in excitement.

Righteous soul living "it shares time with other, help other and doing real love other" then itself is origin of excitement, living in righteous soul living then, it must be righteous soul me is living in "peace and silent of excitement".

Truly macro concept world

Living structures are "righteous soul + wicked soul + mind + body" so that righteous soul with body, of living in righteous soul of being "peace and silent of excitement", here is true is righteous soul living is "peace and silent living".

"Righteous soul + body" then it is must be infer of righteous soul living in destination place, body is shelter of righteous soul, so that in this "righteous soul + body" truly body is shelter only, so that body with righteous soul is micro cosmos.

Righteous soul living under the "peace and silent" Righteous soul get "creature of knowledge" which is help righteous soul livings running to the righteous soul living in destination place.

Righteous soul living of peace and silent is real living; there is no dust and noise. Macro concept world of body is shelter, and then it must be living in righteous soul is master manage body with then, righteous soul body be feel in excitement of peace and silent.

Macro concept world living

"Righteous soul living time and space is peace and silent"

Then macro concept world living is real living.

Macro concept world of righteous soul living also "gentle living, kind and sacrifice and warm behavior"

All macro concept worlds living all actors are same "righteous soul" are living in the body.

To be living in righteous soul living is mind is $1/\infty$, wicked soul is also $1/\infty$

Then it must be living "righteous soul + body= righteous soul body" living then the living is feeling in excitement of peace and silent.

Truly writing time I feel in righteous soul sometimes doing meditation then I feel of righteous soul of peace and silent living.

All of macro concept world living actors do possible living in righteous soul living,

Do live as righteous soul of peace and silent excitement.

Righteous soul sees creature original characteristics

Righteous soul living in excitement with seeing creature original characteristics, Righteous soul is in all of creatures in macro concept world.

Righteous soul and creature original characteristics are living in mind=$1/\infty$.

Living in creature giving original living ways running, original characteristic living way is keep straight on creature creating purpose living.

Creature purpose living me is poor, hard, beggar living role, if that is original characteristics then the way is righteous soul me living.

Then the original characteristics living is there is no energy but the living is running to the righteous soul living in destination living place.

This living if living in poor then, creator really care of me, because righteous soul living in destination place is safe reach at character is must be "wicked soul" Hate living that is "poor living" so that in the creator has given me best character.

But in the mind level living with mind=∞, getting much more than other is distance macro concept world like living is all to be rich living, then original characteristic of the poor is so reluctance to live on, so that originality poor living actor try to be" mind=∞", getting much more than other, then the poor living of righteous soul to be captured by wicked soul, so that "the poor living of original characteristics" are disappeared in the line to running for the righteous soul living in destination place.

"The poor & righteous soul" of "creature original characteristics" then in the righteous soul living in destination place righteous soul living behavior is "it shares time with other, help other, but also doing real love other" then, surviving of "the poor & righteous soul" living is never being worry, because the living of "the poor & righteous soul" living is in cosmos orbit so that righteous soul living in destination place keep watching righteous soul living actor voyage.

Macro concept world "the poor & righteous soul" is hard living in" wicked soul", and mind level living actors.

But righteous soul living is excitement, because righteous soul living is supplied from righteous soul living in destination place keep doing broadcasting so that righteous soul living in "original characteristics" this living is real living and feeling in excitement.

Who knows "the poor & righteous soul" living is "peace and silent of excitement", this living is free from wicked soul and mind slaver. Just living in righteous soul, then this living is creator design living course running to the righteous soul living in destination place, just watching with righteous soul living eye, then the living is come true in the micro concept world living in righteous soul living in destination place.

"Righteous soul sees creature original characteristics"

Living in righteous soul me see a pine tree, righteous soul me see "living in original characteristic living in pine tree"

The tree lived on creature designed living, as to get sun energy all of braches are all go round but there is no straight branch, the tree original living is follow sunshine, so that the living shown to me, tree effort to live, but also righteous soul me see in the state of "mind $1/\infty$, wicked soul$1/\infty$", just perfect righteous soul me living in " original characteristic me" so then righteous soul me and living in pine tree original characteristics then, righteous soul me all being macro concept world creature living.

The tree was same with now macro concept world, as righteous soul me see, righteous soul living pine trees.

Righteous soul of living in "creator designed original character" then see other creature of living each other see as in the micro concept world righteous soul living in destination place living in excitement.

"Creature original characteristics" are all living from birth to grow overcome of temptation by mind and wicked soul, hard living because do not living of wicked soul behavior of easy living, and mind living of gesture of rich, so then the poor of righteous soul living in originality characteristics but righteous soul living all overcomes then the living is how excitement but also to be seen other living of "Righteous soul sees creature original characteristics" how feel in excitement. Keep living is real living of cosmos voyage righteous soul safe returning to the righteous soul living in destination place, then all of care of righteous soul living sous are all excitement.

As living "creature original characteristics" then creator of righteous soul living in destination place living souls are all excitement, this is creators excitement is even survive righteous soul, but righteous soul mission " righteous soul make wicked soul be righteous soul" this greatest mission clear then, the creature of righteous soul is how feel excitement.

Righteous soul living in creator designed characteristic, do not invader other living course, but living ordained creator designed living without any being temptation from wicked soul and mind, just all of living in creator designed characteristic living, this living is real living and survive living even in the macro concept world mixed with wicked soul and mind but, living in creature designed living, then jut as micro concept world righteous soul living of same living possible, so that survived safe returning to the righteous soul living in destination place.

But living in wicked soul and mind living is do not know their lost righteous soul living in destination place "Righteous soul sees creature original characteristics" so that wicked soul and mind follow "thinking of wicked soul" so that wicked soul and mind do not know "creature original characteristics" so that their living is invader other living running line so that others are making hard living, so both other living voyage out of cosmos voyage orbit, so that being disappeared from righteous soul living running to the righteous soul living in destination place.

"Righteous soul sees creature original characteristics" righteous soul living in survive keep traveling voyage in the cosmos then the living is huge in excitement.

See other of living in "creature original characteristics" the living harvest then, the living is art, but also the living is righteous soul consolation each other, before returning to the righteous soul living in destination place, macro concept world living, the living in original characteristics are all to be feeling in excitement.

All to be excitement from macro to micro, it don't have to worry from body living to soul living, because righteous soul living keep voyage orbit to righteous soul living in destination place, so that judgement of unit breath decision action judgement all to be lived as the cosmos law kept so that the living is living in righteous soul living "it shares time with other, help other, but also doing real love other".

"Righteous soul sees creature original characteristics" righteous soul me excitement but also other righteous soul living excitement, but also righteous soul living sous are all excitement.

Righteous soul voyage on macro concept world time

Righteous soul created from righteous soul living in destination place, living in righteous soul living in destination place.

That is time is eternity living, the place is 01234567890, then it must be before of 0, so that living in righteous soul living is zero (0), so that the time is living in righteous soul, the place there is no time eternity living.

But start voyage to macro concept world, then righteous soul governed "time and space" limit,

Righteous soul meet wicked before come to macro concept world, and then it begins righteous soul problems.

Righteous soul with wicked soul from micro concept world, this soul meet mind with body.

Then righteous soul voyage is "righteous soul + wicked soul + mind+ body" then, by turning make clear,

So that it must be infer that as mind=$1/\infty$, then time is required but righteous soul have a time and space as the master living in the macro concept world.

So that it is possible righteous soul of master under the time limit, in the macro concept world.

It is very urgent, righteous soul living is must be living diligent living required, because righteous soul make clear of making "righteous soul + body"= righteous soul body, then here is body is shelter so that righteous soul living being as time floor, then the poor & righteous soul" to reach at "righteous soul & nothing".

To be "righteous soul + body", this living is how to do, wicked soul of wicked behavior and mind of getting much more than other, this is out of these wicked soul mind, so that, righteous soul must free form these living in micro concept cosmos, so that righteous soul living in "the poor & righteous soul".

It must be this is begins 01234567890, then 123..., this is macro concept world, it must be micro concept world is before begins at macro concept world "0" and after all living macro concept world righteous soul safe returning to the righteous soul living in destination place then final zero "0".

As this righteous soul living on time, but also righteous souls climb higher living, but also go deeper of profound deep living place. To go deepest place is to being make clear of all of wicked soul and mind, because wicked soul and mind do not go profound depth. But also huge high place is also easy living of wicked soul, just only getting much more than other livings do not reach at highest place is righteous soul living, it also righteous soul living is to be make clear of wicked soul and mind, so that righteous soul living must do diligence living, for that in the macro concept world, living in righteous soul see before living as righteous soul living actors but also must important is righteous soul living is living in righteous soul, then the condition of righteous soul living is hearing broadcasting from righteous soul living in destination place.

Righteous soul living hearing broadcasting is getting creation of knowledge to run righteous soul living in destination place, so that how to hear is go deeper and go highest then while as the wicked soul and mind doing not reaching time and space then, it can be hear of broadcasting from righteous soul living in destination place.

Righteous soul living is voyage in micro concept of cosmos, so that righteous soul must keep a rule of law of cosmos, so that righteous soul voyage is possible in the orbit to the righteous soul living in destination place.

Righteous soul living with wicked soul and mind level living actor in the macro concept world, then righteous soul living actor used up of time with other wicked soul and mind level living actor, then it is the charity to the wicked soul and mind level living actor, so long, righteous soul living mission safe from wicked soul and mind level living actor to make righteous souls.

Just do living with using "doing real love other" so that wicked soul and mind to be living of righteous soul by the change; just like mutation from wicked soul and mind to righteous soul, so then righteous soul living is doing righteous soul living behavior "it shares time with other, help other, but also doing real love other".

So that time is floor,

Righteous soul living actor do is keep a rule of cosmos law, so that while living in the macro concept world, being break law of cosmos law then, very fast sent to law court judgement, while in the macro concept world living then, keep a rule and clear of breaking rule, all of breaking rule with "think of wicked soul" as the if righteous soul me living follow "thinking of wicked soul" then sure of result is breaking cosmos law, then at first forgive "thinking of wicked soul" then to be clear of breaking rule, then " sent me to the cosmos law court" then I pray please forgive me.

This living is righteous soul living.

It must be righteous souls are 012345678~9 0" then as the runs to the righteous soul living in destination place all of high problems must be solve, so that how to solve then, this is all combined with wicked soul and mind, then to solve the problems, righteous soul keep going up and going deepest place, wicked soul and mind do not reach then help from righteous souls, by hearing broadcasting from righteous soul living in destination place.

Righteous soul are running to the righteous soul living in destination place then, cosmos law orbit voyage then keep guided by righteous soul living in destination place, then righteous soul living safe returning to the righteous soul living in destination place, 01234567890,. Final "0" then it must be all of living followed.

"Righteous soul voyage on macro concept world time" do living in righteous soul living is reaching at righteous soul living in destination place.

Printed in the United States
By Bookmasters